THE THEORY OF SOCIAL CHANGE

THE THEORY OF
SOCIAL CHANGE

Four Views Considered

JOHN McLEISH

SCHOCKEN BOOKS · NEW YORK

Published in U.S.A. in 1969
by Schocken Books Inc.
67 *Park Avenue, New York, N.Y.* 10016

Copyright © *John McLeish* 1969

Library of Congress Catalog Card No. 73–77571

Printed in Great Britain

PREFACE

This short study is intended to be read by students in departments of social studies, education and social psychology in Universities and Colleges of Education. It is an attempt to expound four theories of social change of contemporary significance, and to indicate to the student some of the criteria which might be used in evaluating them. Some care has been taken to avoid dogmatism, either in attempting to force a too-ready assent or a curt dismissal of what are complex and elaborate viewpoints. The author accepts John Stuart Mill's dictum that all views are to be listened to attentively, since no one is capable of grasping the absolute truth on any subject, whereas all human beings can see different aspects or parts of its totality. Especially in assessing the four theories of society and social change must this principle be adopted: there is a certain complementarity and comprehensiveness about these theories which should silence the callow armchair critic and demand considered thought before passing judgement on them.

John McLeish

CONTENTS

BIOGRAPHICAL NOTES

Karl Marx (1818–1883) was born in Prussia, the son of a Jewish lawyer who was converted to Protestantism when Marx was a child. After a brilliant school and university career (Trier High School, Universities of Bonn and Berlin: Ph.D. 1841), Marx found it impossible to obtain a University post because of his radical opinions and Jewish origins. After a brief career as editor of several newspapers (which were successively suppressed by the censors) and after being expelled from France, Marx settled in London where he died in 1883.

In his theoretical views Marx was the first of the modern Communists, developing the characteristic and basic theories of economic determinism, social revolution, and the levelling of class distinctions. The main influences on his thought were successively: Hegelian dialectical philosophy, French Utopian socialism, and British political economy (Adam Smith, Ricardo and others). For many years he was the intellectual prompt of the revolutionary movement in most countries with a decultured and exploited working class (Germany, France, Russia) and attempted to guide the proletarian masses of all countries to revolution by means of the First International which he founded in London in 1864. He played a large part in interpreting, inspiring or justifying the revolutions of 1848, the Paris Commune of 1871 (which he believed to be the prototype of the Communist revolution and the harbinger of the New Society). He is the main authority on Communist theory and practice in all the countries of Eastern Europe, China, and Cuba where Communist revolutions have taken place. Between one-half and one-third of all human beings now living implicitly accept his views as a correct description of reality and of their social condition.

Throughout his life he worked in extremely close comradeship with Friedrich Engels who is the co-founder of Marxism—including the theory of dialectical materialism, social revolution and scientific socialism. Although pressing for the abolition of 'bourgeois marriage', Marx had an extremely happy married life with Jenny von Westphalen (from 1843). She was descended from the 9th Earl of Argyll (Archibald Campbell) who was beheaded by James II of Scotland in 1681. Living often in great poverty in London, the Marx family (father, mother, two daughters and an aged retainer) often survived only by pawning the Argyll silver plate.

FRIEDRICH ENGELS

Friedrich Engels (1820–1895) was born at Barmen in the German Rhineland. He was the son of a cotton manufacturer. After military service he became an active businessman in his father's firm Erman and Engels. He lived in Manchester from 1842 until 1869, when he moved to London. In addition to running a successful business until 1869 and riding regularly to hounds, he worked very closely with Marx in organizing, from England, the revolutionary movement abroad. He wrote a great number of books and articles on the theory of socialism, on military strategy in the revolution, on philosophy and on social questions. Several of these texts have become classics: *The Condition of the Working Class in England in 1844*, *The Military Question and the German Working Class* (1865), *Germany: Revolution and Counter-Revolution* (1851).

Like Marx, Engels could read and speak several languages. For his work in the international revolutionary movement, he equipped himself not only with a knowledge of military tactics (fox-hunting he regarded as an excellent way of keeping fit and learning generalship) but he took pains to learn most European languages so as to act as interpreter at conferences and at clandestine meetings in England with political refugees. Along with Richard Wagner, he participated in the Baden insurrection of 1849—otherwise he saw no active service in the revolutionary battles on the continent.

Like Marx, Engels eventually gave up the idea that the English working class would carry through a Communist-inspired revolution although his interest in this possibility revived when the London Dock Strike broke out in 1889. Engels lived for many years with an Irish girl, Lizzie Burns whom he married in 1864. In periods of special hardship he supported the Marx family so that Karl Marx would be free to write his great work *Das Kapital*. On Marx's death he devoted himself to the task of editing and writing sections of the third volume of this socialist classic. Although having little real influence on the development of the (allegedly) revolutionary parties on the continent during their lifetime—and even less on British political developments—the views of Marx and Engels, when developed by their Russian disciple Vladimir Ilyitch Ulianov (Lenin) now represent an established orthodoxy in all countries where Communist governments are in power.

BRONISLAW MALINOWSKI

Professor Bronislaw Malinowski (1884–1942) was born in Cracow in Poland. He was trained in physical chemistry before coming to London, but changed over to cultural anthropology under the influence of the psychologist Wilhelm Wundt. He spent long periods, during his tenure of the chair of anthropology in the University of London (at the London School of Economics), carrying out field work in New Guinea and Melanesia. He also studied the Hopi Indians in Arizona, some Australian aboriginal tribes, the Chagga of East Africa and the Zatopec Indians of Mexico. It was especially his work on the Trobriand Islanders, on whom he published many distinguished works, which gave him a world reputation as a close observer of the lives and culture of primitive peoples.

He spent some time in America, lecturing at various universities. A number of his theoretical works have been published from manuscripts, posthumously.

SIGMUND FREUD

Sigmund Freud (1856–1939) was born of Jewish parents in Freiberg, a small town in Moravia, then part of the Austro-Hungarian Empire. After a brilliant school career, he studied medicine at the University of Vienna, specializing in physiology. A University research post provided opportunities for work in neurology, but was so badly paid that Freud decided to go into medical practice as a neuro-psychiatrist. He studied hysteria and hypnotism in Paris for a year and on returning to Vienna invented the method of 'free association' which marks the beginning of the psychoanalytic movement.

In spite of intense disapproval by his medical colleagues, he continued to investigate the sexual life and fantasies of the mentally ill patients who came to him in greater and greater numbers. Over a period of thirty years he investigated many problems of the psychic life and wrote many books presenting the psychoanalytic view of neurosis, civilization, prehistory, aesthetics, war, religion and many other major topics.

He was placed in a concentration camp by the Nazis as an enemy of civilization in 1938. Göring accepted a bribe of one million silver dollars subscribed by a devoted follower of Freud's, Princess Buonaparte, and allowed Freud to escape to London where he died in 1939.

G. RATTRAY TAYLOR

G. Rattray Taylor is a writer who specializes in presenting modern scientific knowledge to an educated readership. Amongst his writings are *Sex in History*, the *Angel-Makers*, several texts on biological science. Recently he has specialized in working on scientific scripts for BBC TV.

TALCOTT PARSONS

Talcott Parsons was born in 1902. After graduating in America he studied under Hobhouse and Malinowski at the London School of Economics. His doctoral dissertation (Heidelberg 1925) was on the nature of capitalist society. Returning to America he taught economics and later sociology at Amherst (his own alma mater) and Harvard University. In 1946 he became Chairman of the Department of Social Relations at Harvard. He spent a year as visiting professor (1953–1954) at Cambridge University, England. Parsons is particularly interested in the more obscure religious sects, although he has written distinguished theoretical works on the nature of society, on the relationships between sociology and economics and on a variety of more mundane topics. Under his leadership a distinguished team of scholars have made massive contributions to scholarship, especially in the field of social psychology, group dynamics and sociological theory.

MARXISM AND THE DIALECTICS
OF SOCIAL CHANGE

The basic concern of Marxism is with social change: its primary interest lies in discovering ways of effectively transforming human relations. At the outset of his career as a thinker, when he was still a student, Marx wrote in one of his notebooks a particularly pregnant sentence (freely translated):

'Philosophers have so far only changed their interpretation of the world; the point however is to change the world.'[1]

The massive body of Marxist writing since then can be regarded as being nothing more than a gigantic attempt to understand the implications of this statement.

The problem of evaluating Marxism as a theory of social change crystallizes around the fact that crucial tests, in the form of attempts to apply the basic theory to definitive cases, are lacking. The main concern of Marxist thinkers seems to be to establish, in the most general way, the leading role of economic 'forces' in the dynamic of social change. They seem to be concerned with 'History' and 'Society', rather than with local changes and particular human groups which could provide a scientifically-based test of the theory. Hegel's *World Spirit* and *Absolute Idea* are reduced in status, certainly, to the extent that they lose their initial capital letters. But the vagueness and the generality of the Hegelian dialectic persists in Marxist writings, tending to obscure the explanation of the actual dynamics of particular social and historical changes. This is admitted by Engels, who writes:

'The development of the materialist conception in regard to a single historical example was a scientific work which would have demanded years of tranquil study. . . .'[2]

The conditional mood concedes that the task was never completed. Indeed it was never seriously taken in hand by the founders of historical materialism. Marx's polemical

---

[1] Engels, F., *Ludwig Feuerbach* (1941), p. 73. (Appendix A consists of Marx's eleven 'theses' on Feuerbach.)

[2] Ibid., p. 94.

writings on French history (the Revolution of 1848; the Paris Commune) represent the nearest the founders of Marxism came to approaching this task.

(In Marxism we are dealing with a sociological theory which has many of the characteristics of an *a priori* judgement. The theory seems to be confirmed by certain empirical indications, but it has never been established in detail by a rigid application of the inductive method which is characteristic of sociological investigations. It is *deductive* rather than *inductive* in its essential features.)

(The history of Marx's theory of social innovation makes this *a priori* character clear. The starting point was Hegel. Religious thinkers before him (for example, Augustine) had attempted to establish a pattern in history and the classical Greek writers had developed a cyclical theory to explain historical events.) But Hegel was the first thinker to attempt to produce a *detailed* and *general* theory of the evolution and inner coherence of history. Marx's contribution consisted in completing the translation into secular terms of the Christian explanation of history which remains implicit in Hegel's picture of the development of the cosmos. The universe as a system of interconnected and ever-changing parts ('matter in motion') was seen by Marx to be the real existential basis of all human history and the precondition of social development. Instead of the stage-by-stage progression of Hegel's *Absolute Idea* (a Teutonic circumlocution for 'God') we have the idea of *progress* which operates through a dialectical conflict to be found as a universal principle at the roots of being, the basis of which is material existence. It is a conception of development from the most simple to the most complex. According to Marx's view, there is an impulse *within matter itself* which drives everything towards change. He speaks of 'a tension', 'a vital spirit', and he even feels driven in spite of his scientific approach to use the language of mysticism (Böhme's 'qual')[1] to convey the essence of the question. Matter is, as it were, *in torture*; to escape it must jump from one level of development to another. He quotes the theologian Duns Scotus with approval for asking, as early as the thirteenth century, whether it was possible *for matter to think*.[2] According to Marxism, it is this inner dialectic, this apparant contradic-

---

[1] Engels, F., *Ludwig Feuerbach* (1941), p. 85.   [2] Ibid., p. 85.

tion, which is the motive force, at the very roots of reality, which leads to change. Change is of the essence of all things, and of the relations between things.

The general laws of cosmic development which Marx took over from Hegel need not detain us at this point: we have in mind the 'laws' of quantity into quality; contradiction as the basis of change; the negation of the negation; and so on. These laws certainly function in Marx's social theories because he regards social development as merely one special level of cosmic change. But they take on a specific form in the particular context of human society. At this level, individual human beings and human groups appear on the historical stage as unconscious agents of the historical process. The impulse towards change arises objectively—outside of human awareness and intention ('matter in motion'). But these impulses towards change, and the conditions of change, are 'reflected' in human consciousness as thoughts, feelings, instincts and volitions. This is the *human sensuous activity* of which Marx speaks in his first 'thesis' or declaration on Feuerbach's philosophy.[1] This human activity too is a form of 'matter in motion'. But the objective factors of change, reflected in consciousness, have a subjective bias imposed on them which can be described in such terms as 'ideology', 'ideal tendencies', a 'false consciousness'—some sort of gap between human perceptions and existent social reality. Marx recognizes the existence of two sets of laws which are identical in substance but which differ markedly in their mode of expression. The first set of laws relate to the development of the external world; the second have to do with the laws of human thought. This means that while social changes are produced by men these changes, to be effective, must conform to hidden laws which operate outside of the will, intention and even consciousness of human beings. Social innovations of all kinds, while they often appear to be the consequences of human intention are, in reality, the outcome of innumerable human wills which are to a considerable extent in conflict with each other. Thus the end-result of innovation has a *quality of capriciousness* or of historical accident. As it appears in its final expression, the particular innovation was intended by no one, and is not fully acceptable to any of the social agents. Thus,

[1] Ibid., p. 73.

social changes of whatever kind they may be have always something of the appearance of happy, or unhappy, accidents. In reality, however, they come into being as a result of historical necessity, in consequence of the operation of inviolable laws. 'What is real is rational and what is rational is real,' says Hegel. Marx re-words this rather ambiguous statement in the sense that that which is necessary comes into being; that which has exhausted any possibility of further development must pass away.[1]

The real driving force of change for the Marxist is located in the economic foundations of society. The level of the productive forces of a given society is said to determine the general level of culture, of knowledge and of ideology.[2] Changes which take place in the economic basis are primary. They depend on scientific laws of a causal, determined character. Economic changes are first in order of time and of importance, they are succeeded by changes in the 'superstructure'. These superstructural changes have to do with *ideas*, such as religion, law, literature, theory. These are mere *reflections* of changes in the basis. The economic order is decisive as regards both the rate and the nature of change in our ideas.

In modern industrial society the main vehicle of social innovation is the class struggle, that is, the struggle of those who live by selling their labour power against those who live by exploiting the labour of the 'have-nots'. Force, as the midwife of social change, is the arbiter between social classes.[3] Reason and human intention play but a small part in determining the outcome of historical confrontations: of more import are the *objective, historically developed* conditions. In particular, the relationship between the 'productive forces' of society and the 'productive relations' are decisive. In this formulation, Marx asserts that the final outcome of historical struggle, which is the crucial factor in social change, is decided by causal laws and relationships which stand outside of human consciousness

[1] Marx-Engels, *Correspondence (1846–1895)* (1936), pp. 310–11, 475, 518; cf. Konstantinov, F. V. (1950, 1954, 1955).

[2] Marx, K., *Critique of Political Economy* (1904), pp. 11–13; cf. Marx, K. and Engels, F., *The German Ideology* (1940), pp. 28–9.

[3] Marx, K. and Engels, F., *The Communist Manifesto* (1935), pp. 10–20; cf. Engels, F., *Le Role de la Violence dans l'Histoire* (1939), p. 130.

and will. These laws and relationships assert themselves in the form of external necessity to which all wills must bow.[1]

It is a general rule or social law that the new is inevitably in conflict with the old. In practice, this means that the social innovator is brought up short, face to face with social traditions, with irrational ideologies, with vested interests which operate together as a great conservative force opposing change.[2] The innovator who is fortunate enough to have the 'forces of history' on his side can overcome resistances to change—but in a fashion which is neither anticipated, nor intended by him. There must inevitably be differences in the degree to which individual innovators are conscious of the objective situation (this includes the productive forces, productive relations, the political struggle, the ideological situation, the next dialectical step forward, etc.). There will also be differences in the degree to which individuals can assimilate their purposes to the general dialectical movement of history. This is what Marx means by 'class consciousness'. Class consciousness implies that a *partisan* approach is essential before we can understand the nature of reality and how desirable changes can be brought about. In direct opposition to liberal thinking, Marxists maintain that the individual must be *involved* in the process of changing reality before he can begin to understand its essential qualities. He who seeks to understand must begin by assuming a position which involves a value-judgement. The social innovator can succeed best if he consciously adopts a class position and a committed standpoint. It is only on this basis that he can begin to understand the relation of class forces, and to be able to predict the immanent movement of productive forces and productive relations in the given historical epoch.[3]

With reference to the particular problem we are concerned with, that is, how social change comes about, one of the central questions is that of the relationship of the intelligentsia or educated classes to the social process. The same must be said about this question, as it has been dealt with by Marxists, as has been already said about the general theory of social change. The detailed relation between the individual and the specific

[1] Engels, F., *Ludwig Feuerbach*, op. cit., pp. 54–5.
[2] Lenin, V. I., *Leninski Sbornik*, vol. 9, pp. 230, 267.
[3] Lenin, V. I., *Sochineniya*, 4th edit., Moscow, 1947, vol. 14, p. 343.

5

innovation for which he may be held 'responsible' (not to say given credit) is left in the obscurity of an abstract and general formulation by Marxist writers. However certain indications are given as to how this question should be answered.

The distinction between basis and superstructure has been indicated. This distinction was first declared in a classic statement by Marx:

'The totality of production relations constitutes the economic structure of society, the real basis upon which a legal and political superstructure arises and to which definite forms of social consciousness correspond. The mode of production of the material means of life determines, in general, the social, political, and intellectual processes of life.'[1]

(This is the doctrine of historical materialism. It asserts that all the ideas, the institutions and the apparent characteristics of a given social system *are determined* by the way in which people gain their livelihood, i.e. by the reigning mode of production.) As a direct corollary, it is declared that the very essence of man in any historical period derives from his relationship to the productive process. 'The human essence is no abstraction inherent in each single individual. In its reality it is the *ensemble* of the social relations.'[2] This can be interpreted to mean that the intellectual who is never, by definition, involved directly in the actual process of production, must remain involved in purely superstructural activities. As a productive social agent he is concerned solely with the manufacture and transmission of ideology. But this fact does not necessarily exclude him from consideration as a social innovator: it is also a principle that the superstructure is not merely a *passive reflection* of the economic basis. It is an active force, it is used by all as an instrument in the class-struggle. On the one side, it is active in defence of the existing relations, on the other it is a pacemaker in the drive to change existing productive relationships.[3] Lenin assigns to ideas the honourable status of *material* forces. He says: '*theory* becomes a *material force* when it has gripped the masses'. (When Marx says that economic relations are primary, and thoughts, feelings and volitions are derivative and secondary

[1] Marx, K., *Critique of Political Economy* (1904), pp. 11–13.
[2] VIth thesis on Feuerbach, in Engels, F., op. cit.
[3] Stalin, J. V., *Concerning Marxism in Linguistics* (1950), p. 4.

he does not mean that the latter are unimportant. Nor does he exclude the possibility of a two-way interaction between economy (the productive basis) and ideas (the ideological superstructure).)It is true that for Marxism, the intelligentsia as a social 'grouping' (they do not constitute a 'class') are less 'fundamental' than workers or entrepreneurs. Human societies have the ability to survive without very much abstract thought: they cannot survive at all without food and primary production. But this does not rule out the possibility that a particular intellectual, at a particular moment of time, may be more valuable to the continuing life of society than an individual entrepreneur, workman, machine or manufacturing process, engaged in primary production of the basic necessities of life. This point is conceded:

'Exchange of ideas is a constant and vital necessity: without this it is impossible to coordinate the actions of people in the struggle against the forces of nature, in the struggle to produce the necessary material values; without it, it is impossible to ensure the success of society's productive activity and hence the very existence of social production becomes impossible'.[1]

Whilst it must be emphasized that Marxism stresses that social life is essentially practical, this is not to be taken as a denigration of theory. The emphasis depends on context. When controverting any tendency towards 'idealism' Marxists insist on the primacy of *action*. But when confronted by mechanical materialism they emphasize the significance of ideals, of abstract thought, of theory as guiding the transforming activity of man in society.[2]

According to Marxism, the basis of all change is contradiction. The law of contradiction, otherwise known as the law of the unity of opposites, is the most basic law of Marxist dialectics. According to Lenin: 'Dialectics in its proper meaning is the study of the contradiction within the very essence of things.' In his philosophical notebooks he quotes from Philo Alexandrinus who, in classical antiquity, had already defined the fundamentals of the Marxist or dialectical way of thinking:

'For is not unity that which is composed of two contraries? Unity is of such a nature that, divided in two, the contraries

---

[1] Ibid., p. 16.
[2] Engels, F., *Anti-Dühring* (no date), Chapter 12.

7

appear. Is this not the very principle which, according to the Greeks, Heraclitus, their great and celebrated philosopher, recognized as the cornerstone of his philosophy and which he boasted of as a new discovery?'[1]

Marxism agrees with Heraclitus that contradiction is of the essence of all things: it is absolute and universal. Contradiction as the basis of change exists in all processes from the beginning to the end of the development of things. In discussing concrete cases of cosmic, individual or social change, the Marxist method consists in tracing the movement of opposites ('the division of the one and the knowledge of its contradictory Parts . . . the knowledge of the unity of these opposites').[1]

It must be noted however that contradictions are not necessarily *antagonistic* in character. Marxism is essentially a theory of change through conflict, but it recognizes another kind of change which takes place on the basis of non-antagonistic contradictions. Marx recognized this as early as 1845, when he was 27 years old. But the point has been stated very clearly in modern times by one of his leading disciples:

'Contradiction and struggle are universal and absolute. But the way we set about solving contradictions, in other words, the forms of struggle, differ according to differences in the nature of the contradictions. Some contradictions are marked by the existence of open antagonism, some are not. When we consider the concrete development of things, some contradictions which are originally non-antagonistic change and become antagonistic: some contradictions which are originally antagonistic, change and become non-antagonistic.'[2,3]

When we are thinking about social change and trying to identify causes, the basic contradictions we must look for are of three main kinds: contradictions between the productive forces and productive relations; contradictions between the economic basis and the ideological superstructure; and contradictions which may exist within the superstructure itself. We have to remember also that the law of contradiction operates within the sphere of human thinking. This provides us with a

---

[1] Lenin, V. I., *Filosofskiye Tetrady* (1947), p. 263. (Editions Sociales, 1955, p. 279.)
[2] Mao Tse-Tung, *Selected Works* (1954), vol. 2, p. 50.
[3] Text of speech of February 27th, 1957, p. 2.

fourth field of investigation. In studying change, the Marxist method is to identify the *fundamental* contradiction. This provides the key which enables us to interpret and understand the whole movement in Marxist terms. At the same time we must be sensitive to the fact that we are observing a dynamic or ever-changing *process*. This means that we must expect that the principal contradiction will only be such for a limited period; new forms of struggle will appear within the reality we are studying; the unity of opposites will establish itself; the negation will be itself negated, and the new *One* will undergo cleavage into novel elements; antagonistic contradictions will give way to non-antagonistic; there will be an eternal flux. To quote Lenin's philosophical notebooks:

'Dialectics . . . studies how opposites can *be* identical and how they *become* identical (how they change and become identical)—under what conditions they transform themselves into each other and become identical—why it is that the human mind should not regard these opposites as dead, rigid things, but as living, conditional, changeable entities which transform themselves into each other.'[1]

In a series of letters written in 1890, 1893 and 1894, Engels amplifies and qualifies the cardinal principles of historical materialism stated above, as these are given by Marx. In letters to Schmidt, to Mehring, and to Starkenburg he defines more precisely the kinds of interaction and processes which operate in the production of ideology.[2] This is a basic concept which must be understood before the Marxist view of social realities can be grasped in its fulness. The distinction between economic basis and superstructure is reiterated by Engels in these letters. The fundamental law: that *the mode of production ultimately determines philosophical, religious, artistic and literary concepts* is not withdrawn. But several important qualifications are added. These are so fundamental that a completely new emphasis is involved. The theory of historical materialism at this point takes on a flexibility and subtlety which is appropriate to the complexity of interactions in human groups.

Engels' analysis begins with the mode of production. By this

---

[1] Lenin, V. I., op. cit., p. 76 (French edit., p. 90), cf. Engels, F., *Dialectics of Nature*, 1940.
[2] Marx-Engels, *Correspondence*, pp. 477–84, 510–12, 516–19.

he means particular productive processes, machines, labour power, the level of technical development, the prevailing mode of distribution, and all other material relationships which appertain to the satisfaction of the *physical needs* of a given society. The mode of production, so defined, constitutes the economic basis. There are certain fundamental laws which operate at this level completely independently of human will and consciousness. These laws and these productive relationships *ultimately* determine the character of all other social and personal relationships.

As the first stage in such causal determinations, certain 're-flexes' or 'reflections' of the economic basis come into being. First of all, within the mode of production itself we can find at an early stage, a certain development of the division of labour which produce divergencies of interest. But at the same time, certain *common* social functions have still to be carried out if the society is to survive. These basic social needs give rise to a class of functionaries who are selected, or who select themselves, to carry out these common functions within the social context of the division of labour. Engels refers here to the functions of social book-keeping, marking off the calendar to establish the seasons, safeguarding the sacred and profane lore of the group, and so on. However, inevitably these common functionaries develop interests which are distinct from those of the productive group. It becomes their self-appointed task to render themselves (politically) independent of those who gave them office. It is in this way that the State comes into being, according to Engels. The State is the first 'reflection' of the economic basis. It is rather unfortunate that the word 'reflection' (a key word in Marxist epistemology and the theory of social process) is never adequately defined. In this context Engels explains that the 'reflections' of the economic base are analogous to those in the human eye. The image in the retina is produced by light passing through a converging lens: this inverts the image. Reality appears upside down, things seem to be standing on their heads. Now, the nervous system (which in the case of human sight, serves to re-invert the image) is missing in the social process. By means of this crude metaphor, which defies any literal or scientific interpretation, Engels means to convey to us the idea that the *real* relations between the State and production (namely, that State functionaries are parasitic on primary producers) are turned the wrong way round. In other words, the State appears to be primary, the productive processes secondary. This seems to the participants to be so, not only as far as function but also as far as historical sequences are concerned. This kind of fantastic reflection of reality is exactly what we mean by the word 'ideology'.

The conflict of interest which arises at this early stage between primary producers and State functionaries manifests itself first of all as a political struggle. But this struggle is extremely obscure in its nature because it too appears in an 'inverted' or reflected form. The direct struggle for control of the means of production, the struggle between the two social classes which have now emerged, is transformed into a political struggle. This political struggle is merely an inverted and fantastic reflection of the class-struggle which goes on at the ultimate level of economic production. The political struggle, at least at this stage of social development, is a kind of shadow-boxing.

'On the whole, the economic movement gets its way. But it has to suffer repercussions from the political movement which it established and which it endowed with relative independence: it is affected by movements of the state power on the one hand and of the opposition which this engenders on the other.'[1]

According to Engels' account, we can distinguish in logical succession the same kind of natural development whereby the relatively independent fields of law, religion, philosophy and science are thrown up in the course of this struggle. Although these are primarily reflections of the economic basis, they begin to lead a *relatively* independent life, mutually interacting and influencing each other. They also interact with the economic basis. The nature and quality of the interactions between different parts of the superstructure, between basis and superstructure, between different parts of the economic basis, alter through time. One cannot specify in advance which particular sections will interact. Nor can we say which will be the dominant sources of influence, nor what the particular outcome will be. Each concrete case must be studied by the Marxist method, particular decisions must be made, the appropriate action must

[1] Marx-Engels, *Correspondence*, p. 480.

be taken, as involved partisans. The *general* movement of history is plain and the *ultimate* determination of ideology by economic processes and relations certain. But it is anti-dialectical to perceive the economic basis and the ideological superstructure as unchanging and polar opposites. Neither must we stereotype our thinking in terms of the first being cause and the second effect in an absolute sense.

'The whole vast process proceeds in the form of interaction (though of very unequal forces, the economic movement being by far the strongest, most elemental and most decisive)'.[1]

It is of the very nature of ideology (whether it be religious, philosophical, scientific, literary, artistic or the common consciousness) that the real relationships between phenomena remain unknown. As we have seen, these relationships normally appear in an inverted form. Ideology is a conscious process but it proceeds on the basis of a false consciousness. It is characteristic of the production of ideological material that we engage in thinking without being aware of the remote processes which actually determine our thought content. Since the *actual* determinants of social action must remain forever unknown to the ideologist, false determinants are invented. In other words, the sources of social innovation can be perceived only in a more or less fantastic reflection, topsy-turvy, upside-down. Thus, for example, religious conceptions, philosophical ideas, literary insights, artistic expression, scientific models, share the characteristic that they are falsely regarded by those who hold them as entities which require no explanation other than that they exist. Engels concedes that ideological constructs have a certain relative autonomy, indeed that they may even influence economic processes. But they manifest a basic topsy-turvydom, inherent in the fact that they have their being merely as economic reflexes, where everything is upside down. It is a fact that ideology reacts on the economic basis to modify it: but it is more important to note that *in the last analysis* the mode of production is primary, ideology secondary; that the economic basis will have its way. Recognition of this reality is what distinguishes Utopianism from Science.

Within the realm of ideology itself we can discover a reality-irreality dimension. Religion and philosophy soar higher than

[1] Marx-Engels, *Correspondence*, p. 484.

law, politics and science. This is for two reasons: the relationship between religion and philosophy and the economic reality is more tenuous; and (in Engels' phrase) philosophy and religion have inherited a greater store of prehistoric '*bunk*'. At this point he introduces an unexplained concept: he maintains that the false conceptions of religion and philosophy (spirits, magical forces, erroneous views of nature and of man's being) arise in prehistoric times on a 'negative economic basis'.[1] These false ideas tend to influence production negatively, and act to maintain it at a lower level. This *may* mean that productive resources are diverted from social use to satisfy particular deities, or to furnish the last resting place of kings. It is difficult to understand what a 'negative economic basis' means, unless this is Engels' way of saying that the various categories of magic, of spirits, of deities, are *spontaneously* produced. Such an idea is absolutely contrary to the basic conceptions of Marxism. Again, he makes another assertion which seems to contradict his basic assumptions, that 'it would be pedantic surely to attempt to find economic causes for all this primitive nonsense'.[2]

In spite of the emphasis on the *irrational* character of ideology Marxism insists that society is made up of conscious agents who work with deliberation and passion towards definite goals.[3] Social change is not a product of blind, impersonal forces. It is the result of the meeting of innumerable human wills and actions. Nothing happens without a conscious purpose, without an intended human aim. But it must be observed that it is not a *particular* human will which determines the force of events. It is this which makes social changes appear to have a chance or capricious quality about them. The general will is a kind of average decision which is not desired by any single agent.[4] Therefore chance appears to reign. But 'chance' itself is made up of a multiplicity of causes, mostly unknown, each contributing a small amount to the general effect. Causality reigns, but the nature of the laws of social development remains unknown to the participants. They are conscious only of the contrast between their intentions and the general result.[5] The causal

---

[1] Ibid., p. 482.   [2] Ibid.
[3] Engels, F., *Ludwig Feuerbach*, op. cit., p. 58.
[4] Marx-Engels, *Correspondence*, p. 518.
[5] Cf. Letter to Bloch, ibid., pp. 475-7.

relationship between event and pre-determining causes must be determined by an analysis of each concrete situation. Marxism enables us to say in a general way that analysis will be most profitable if we start from the development of productive forces. The character of class relations; the inter-relations between ideological constructs and between these and the economic basis; the balance of class forces—these are the most significant elements of the total situation to which attention must be directed at a very early stage. Individual participants in the social process are to be regarded as representative of a class, and of a class interest. They may be more or less consciously aware of their economic interest and allegiance, but at the same time they are prone to all kinds of superstructural fantasies. These work in such a way as to obscure the character of the social process in which all are involved. They also obscure, in greater or less degree, the relationship between social acts and class interest.[1]

The Marxist theory of social change is a formidable intellectual instrument. It has given rise to considerable controversy. Criticism has come from ethical, philosophical, historical, political standpoints, and from many others. It is not proposed to detail these criticisms, nor to evaluate the theory from any general standpoint. Instead of a generalized critique it appears more useful at this stage of development of social theory to accept Marxism as a working model of social change and put it to work. This can be done by testing how far it makes a particular social situation or social innovation comprehensible. In other words, it is appropriate to consider the theory as a contribution to social science, rather than to criticize it in general terms as a political doctrine. It then becomes necessary to test how far the hypotheses and general concepts are valid in particular instances. In making this attempt we accept the basic premise that social science, like every other, advances by attempting to falsify hypotheses by empirical tests, and not as a result of a philosophical critique.

[1] cf. Letter to Bloch, Marx-Engels, *Correspondence*, p. 511.

2

SOCIAL EQUILIBRIUM AND SOCIAL CHANGE: MALINOWSKI'S FUNCTIONALISM

The theory of functionalism, developed by Malinowski, assumes that all social processes are causally determined. In fact, the importance of functionalism in social thought is that it applies the principle of causality to every element of culture without exception. Culture is to be understood in the anthropological sense as including customs, traditions, institutions, material artefacts, symbolism. According to Malinowski's theory, nothing that belongs to this system is the result of capricious invention. Every item is causally justified. This is the case because before any new thing can be incorporated in the cultural system, it must satisfy some human need. The need may be *simple*, being derived directly from our nature as living organisms, or it may be a more complex, derived need. The first appearance, and the continued survival, of any innovation in the cultural system is therefore part of the same universal lawful process[1] which simultaneously binds the stars in their courses and ensures that Westernized males wear black ties with dinner jackets.

The most important determinant is the law of survival. Malinowski says:

'No crucial system of activities can persist without being connected, directly or indirectly, with human needs and their satisfaction. The understanding of any cultural element must imply, among other things, the statement of its relationships, instrumental or direct, to the satisfaction of essential needs . . . The imperfection in technical performance, the disobedience of the rules of cooperation, and the mishandling of objects or people, in short, provide ultimate punishment of the organism by the miscarriage of the instrumental sequence.'[2]

This could be described as Rousseau's discipline of nature applied to every aspect of human behaviour. It is the Darwinian

[1] Malinowski, B. (1960), p. 142   [2] Ibid., p. 41.

principle of natural selection generalized in such a way that it acts on whole societies and on each single element of group culture. It is Bentham's principle of utility writ large so as to account for the continued survival of cultural artefacts in social life and to explain their disappearance when their utility is exhausted.

From the practical point of view the importance of functionalism is that it provides an analytical scheme by means of which we can undertake a systematic analysis of any society, or of any social institution.[1] Malinowski's scheme of analysis is both comprehensive and relevant. The analytical categories can be used to analyse both stationary and dynamic social systems. The anatomy and physiology of the social system are made plain. Each element finds its place in the total economy of the social system.

Malinowski takes the unit of cultural analysis to be the institution.[2] This means that an analysis of a culture could begin by exhaustively listing the institutions to be found in it— such things as family organization, age groupings, 'uplift groups', caste systems, city organizations, secret societies, and so on. These can be taken as representing the social molecules. Further breakdown by means of the functionalist scheme can provide us with a complete picture of the functioning society—provided we include a description of the inter-relationships of these various institutions within the social system. The existence of any institution depends on the agreement amongst its members on a set of values. These are usually of a traditional character (as is the case, for example, in the family). The values constitute one way of defining the aims and purposes for which the human beings associated with the institution have come together. The institution will also have some sort of structure. This means that the individuals in question stand in definite relationships to each other and to specific physical parts of the environment.[3]

Each institution is analysed in terms of categories which have been arrived at on the basis of certain methodological assumptions: taken together these assumptions add up to a kind of

[1] Malinowski, B. (1960), pp. 53, 141; cf. Malinowski, B. (1945).
[2] Ibid., pp. 52 ff.; (1945), p. 50.
[3] Ibid., pp. 162–7, 110.

social behaviourism. The analytical scheme which is derived from this scientific approach to culture seeks relentlessly to substitute *objectively* determinable factors for subjectively based ones. Thus it concerns itself with social action and the objective results of action, and not at all with individual motives. The functionalist seeks for general laws which will bind together the largest possible number of facts. These facts are discovered *not* by speculative cogitations on introspective data, but by *observation* and *experiment* on overt behaviour in a defined area. The initial and major problem in this kind of scientific enterprise is to discover some method of controlling and limiting academic discourse. The purpose of this control operation is to ensure that the conclusions drawn will be based on systematic, empirical work which describes an external reality, rather than on literary elegance and sophistication which may lack any reality check. Malinowski says in this connection:

'Each scientific theory must start from and lead to observation. It must be inductive, and it must be verifiable by experience. In other words, it must refer to human experiences which can be defined, which are public, that is, accessible to any and every observer, and which are recurrent, hence fraught with inductive generalizations, that is, predictive.'[1]

This statement is to be interpreted to mean that in describing a culture by means of some analytical scheme, we must take our starting point *not* from the exotic, sensational or outlandish elements—a method which would not be a scientific approach however appropriate it may be to the traveller's tale or journalistic method. Rather we must begin from the ordinary everyday satisfaction of man's most elementary needs. Our task is to relate these needs and their satisfaction to the organized behaviour of human beings in a social situation, and to the type of social structure prevailing. '*Man does not live by bread alone, but he lives primarily by bread.*'[2]

Having moved away from our starting point, we should next consider the more complex, derived and indirect needs. These are just as imperative as the basic biological ones. Logically they may be secondary, historically they may be derivative; but the method of science consists in relating these economic, or social, or spiritual needs (and their satisfaction) to the basic

[1] Malinowski, B. (1960), p. 67.   [2] Ibid., p. 72.

needs, and both to a system of general laws of an explanatory character.[1] This does not at all imply that we are forced to reduce the economic, social and spiritual imperatives to the biological needs of eating, sleeping, drinking, copulating and defaecating. On the contrary: the biological needs and the ways in which they are satisfied are caught up in a plexus of social forms, traditions, customs, mythologies, sanctions, and so on. According to Malinowski's view, no piece of human behaviour is ever spontaneous (in the sense of 'natural'): we eat, drink, sleep and the rest according to certain modes which have become 'fashionable' in our type of society. The functionalist approach does not claim to predict how any problem will be solved in any particular cultural setting, as biology can predict how basic needs will be satisfied by a given species of animal in a state of nature. What it does say is that human problems, which are essentially *social* in character, will be solved by cultural responses, since these problems are both universal and categorical. Cultural imperatives derive from three sets of conditions: these are: biological necessity, environment, and the cultural responses already in existence. It is very far from Malinowski's intention to reduce all cultural data to a crude scheme of response to simple biological urges. Nor does he seek to separate the material aspects of social behaviour from the symbolic. He is willing to recognize such things as 'consciousness', 'ideas', 'spiritual realities', 'values', 'thoughts', 'ideals', 'beliefs' and so on—but only provided these can be so defined as to be identifiable in overt or, in other words, *observable* behaviour.[2] Words and symbols are real only through their social consequences. The beautiful thought, the song, or the speech which remains unspoken, unsung, unread, or unheard can never be the concern of scientific investigation. Indeed, these have no cultural reality of any kind.

Having defined Malinowski's basic methodological assumptions, let us now consider his analytical scheme. Logically we must begin with the institution since this is the social unit. In analysing any institution it is convenient to begin with the *charter*.[3] This defines the system of values (aims and purposes) for which human beings organize and enter into association

[1] Malinowski, B. (1960), pp. 85 ff., 120 ff.
[2] Ibid., p. 23.   [3] Ibid., pp. 52, 140, 162.

18

within the institution. The charter need not be a written document, in fact rarely is this the case. Nor need individual members be consciously aware of their aims in joining an institution. Indeed, in most cases the individual is not even consulted as to whether he wishes to join, and sanctions will normally be applied if he attempts to leave. We may instance the family as an example here. The charter of marriage (which usually anticipates the family in point of time) normally includes an exclusiveness in sexual intercourse, the procreation of children, property rights, and so on. The institution of the family entails friendly association with other members. This involves companionship, rituals of respect, prescribed forms of address between the various generations in association, and so on. The implications of these various charters are hardly ever subjected to rational scrutiny by members of these institutions. Nor do they give a free assent to the categorical provisions which they have had no part in formulating. We do not ask to be born: neither do we have a choice in the cultural heritage transmitted by our parents. Our choice of marital partner is generally circumscribed and social convention limits us in unforeseen ways after the decision has been made to enter into a contractual relationship. What is certain is that the particular type of family into which we are born, willy-nilly, will be such as will satisfy our basic needs, in the normal case. It will also create new needs and develop new habitual modes of satisfying them. These processes go on largely outside of our conscious awareness. Thus, each of us tends to assume the 'natural' and 'spontaneous' character of what are, in reality, peculiar and specific forms of social institutions which nurture us.

The second analytical category is that of *personnel*.[1] Every human group is organized on the basis of authority. There is some division of function, some pattern of distribution of privileges and duties. These structural elements will normally be closely correlated. For example, a particular type of family has a certain structure based on a hierarchy of rights and duties. Rewards and imperatives of a specific kind are linked to the place of the individual arising from the division of function which enables society and its institutions to survive. The system is buttressed from the effects of radical change by sanctions which

[1] Ibid., pp. 52–66.

are normally attached to any violation of the established rules. These sanctions are applied differentially, depending on one's position in the institutional hierarchy. Every society has, and must have, at its disposal certain mechanisms to ensure that it survives as a group from one generation to another. This is normally ensured by making sure that the specific structures defined in terms of division of labour, of authority, of rights and duties are reproduced along with the ever-changing personnel. Social life is very like that of a complex organism. Individual cells die, to be continually replaced *in situ* by new ones which take over the function of the deceased cells. The processes of anabolism and catabolism work together to ensure that the structures and functioning of the organism in its environment persist without any major change.

The third analytical category defining the institution consists of *rules* or *norms*.[1] These are the technical acquired skills, habits, legal standards, ethical commands, etiquette, and so on, which are accepted by the members of the institution, or which are imposed on them. No social organization exists of itself: every society is embedded in a social and natural environment. It must obtain resources from the environment to satisfy the needs of its personnel. This involves skills and tasks which are carried out in accordance with traditional instrumental sequences and rituals. In its essence, culture is a complex apparatus which places human beings in a more advantageous position in coping with the concrete problems of their environment. It operates in such a way as to transform the satisfaction of needs more and more to a routine process. This routinization acts to conserve human energy: it can come about and be maintained only if each contributes his quantum of effort in accordance with agreed and traditional rules. It is the function of the rules and norms to define the established routines: they define, implicitly and explicity, one's rights and one's duties within the structure of the institution.[2]

Fourthly, there are *activities*.[3] These can be of many kinds and represent concrete types of behaviour generated by the rules, and provided for by the charter. Activities, according to Malinowski, deviate invariably from the rules.[3] This is partly

[1] Malinowski B. (1960), pp. 52–66.
[2] Ibid., pp. 53, 110.   [3] Ibid., p. 53.

because the actual performance depends on the ability, power, honesty and good-will of the members. The rules state the ideal of performance, the activities represent its reality. But the reality must not depart too far and too consistently from the ideal. The limit is defined by the point at which the instrumental sequence fails to be accomplished. This may result where there is a regular failure in the accuracy with which symbols reflect realities: or the failure may be due to the fact that needs remain unsatisfied. Through its activities the group keeps alive the tradition of knowledge, of law and of ethics on which its continuance depends.

The fifth category of conceptual analysis is the *function* of the institution.[1] This is the integral and objective result of organized group activities. In its simplest, and most basic aspect the function of behaviour is the satisfaction of biological impulses by the appropriate acts. In the context of culture (outside of which man is a mere animal) human needs are satisfied by specific activities in which human beings cooperate, use artefacts, and consume goods. Function is closely related to needs. Needs, in turn, are related to ends or *values*. Malinowski reiterates that the most basic value in all cultures is survival. But it is characteristic of humans that their basic needs and the cultural means of satisfying them are linked to new and derived needs,[2] which impose a new and secondary determinism. As stated previously, our physiological needs are satisfied not in natural and spontaneous ways but in accord with new integral culture patterns. These operate in such a way as to unite man, society and culture in a unity which transcends the animal impulse, transforming it into a *cultural* imperative. At this point we might define function as the objective role which the institution plays within the total cultural system. It is akin to the definition a visiting anthropologist might give of the part the institution plays within the total context of the society he is investigating. On the other hand the charter is more like the idea the group itself has of the institution. It is a detailed statement of the things they hope for and expect from the institution. Just as activities diverge from rules, so charter and function never exactly coincide.[3] The discrepancy between them could well be

[1] Ibid., pp. 53, 118–19 *passim.*
[2] Ibid., Chapters 10 and 11.   [3] Ibid., p. 53.

a source of energy available to the social innovator. When the hiatus between what is hoped for and what is actually obtained becomes too great it is to be expected that some members of the group will set out to change the reality closer to the ideal.

Lastly, there is the *material apparatus*. This includes all the elements of material culture; for example, tools, economic system, ornaments, cult impedimenta, and so on.[1] But the material apparatus does not consist merely of objects distributed in certain spatial relationships *vis-à-vis* each other and the personnel of a given society. The physical objects are caught up and transformed by the cultural process. They acquire a certain 'second-hand' appearance, as though no longer fresh from the hands of the Creator but stamped with the impress of human manipulation. They develop a certain aura, a fetishism which distinguishes them from the natural article. They become part of culture: they lose their pristine freshness, never again to recover it.

The relationships between these various categories can be shown in the diagram.

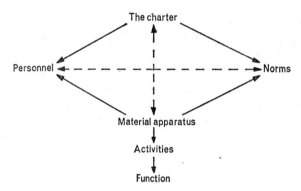

Malinowski sums up these relationships as follows:

'Human beings organize under a charter that defines their common aims and that also determines the personnel and norms of the conduct of the group. Applying these norms and with the use of the material apparatus, the members engage in activities, through which they contribute towards the integral function of the institution.'[2]

[1] Malinowski, B. (1960), pp. 36–42.
[2] Malinowski, B. (1945), p. 43—footnote.

Functionalism can best be understood as the attempt to apply the principle of natural selection to all the elements of culture, without exception. Any system of activities in which human beings involve themselves is linked directly or indirectly with the satisfaction of their needs. On the basis of this understanding, the culture pattern is a closely integrated system of habits which operates so as to produce optimal satisfaction for the minimum expenditure of energy. This is achieved in consequence of the fact that rewarded activities tend to become installed as habitual responses in given situations. On the other hand, failure to reinforce a particular habit by reward causes it to drop out of the repertoire of cultural behaviour. If culture fails to satisfy basic needs one of two things *must* happen: either individuals perish and the society fails to survive, or the culture pattern is modified so as to ensure the minimal satisfaction of basic needs.

The conception of *need* is basic to Malinowski's theory. By this word he understands a set of conditions which are generated in the individual within the context of culture.[1] Need can be understood as a limiting set of constraints which are imposed by the relationship between the individual, his culture, and the natural environment. The most basic needs are organic, biological. Related to these are derived, more complex, and secondary needs which can be grouped under the headings instrumental, recreative and integrative needs. The basic human needs are for food, warmth, shelter, and the satisfaction of certain biological impulses. Under *instrumental* needs we find those imperatives which are classified as economic, normative, educational and political needs. As well as these we have *integrative* imperatives: these include knowledge (science), religion, and magic. The fourth group consists of *recreative* imperatives such as play, art, association, and so on. Of these different categories Malinowski says:

'Any theory of culture has to start from the organic needs of man, and if it succeeds in relating the more complex, indirect, but perhaps fully imperative needs of the type we call spiritual or economic or social, it will supply us with a set of general laws such as we need in sound scientific theory.'[2]

[1] Malinowski, B. (1960), *passim*, but especially pp. 62–5, 91–131.
[2] Ibid., pp. 72–3.

23

This quotation must be interpreted in the sense that man, liberated from the determinism of nature which binds all other animals, becomes the victim, and simultaneously the agent of another determinism: that of culture. At the same time, culture is itself bound within a system of iron laws: the determinism of nature is raised to a higher power. The law of natural selection is abrogated so far as the individual man is concerned. But it operates now on the total social and cultural system within which he is embedded. Any failure in the sequence of habitual activities, for example, failure of cooperation, or the failure to translate relevant natural and social phenomena into group symbols, or failure in the supply of tools, leads inevitably to the gradual extinction of the whole cultural apparatus and with it the human group.[1] This implies that to understand any element of culture we must relate it to the system by which human needs are satisfied within the given group. Culture is a vast apparatus, partly material, partly behavioural, partly spiritual, which develops to enable *Homo sapiens* to cope with the specific and concrete problems posed within the context of survival in a hostile environment. From the hostile environment of nature man attempts to create a second more friendly environment: this is culture itself. It enables him so to work on nature as to procure the essentials for his human needs. At the same time culture creates new demands; simultaneously it ensures that these shall be satisfied also.[2]

Culture is thus an integral and unique achievement of the human species. Each culture is complete and self-sufficient since it must satisfy the range of needs of the individual and of the group. Culture equips us with powers and talents far beyond our isolated individual potentialities. But it imposes certain limitations on our activities and experiences, restrictions foreign to our anthropoid ancestors in a state of nature. In this way social stability is achieved. The group can perform the activities necessary for survival (reproduction and nurture of the new generation, transmission of the culture pattern) only by drastically curtailing the spontaneity of the individual. The omnipotence of the random will is brought within establishment limits in the interests of equilibrium and stability.

Up to this point, Malinowski's theory refers only to social

[1] Malinowski, B. (1960), p. 144.   [2] Ibid., pp. 68–9.

conservation. There seems to be no place in his theoretical system for change, nor any attempt to explain that ubiquitous process. Critics have pointed to this supposed failing of functionalism, having no regard for the fact that such a glaring anomaly must have been obvious also to the perceptive minds of the functionalist school. It is true that the societies Malinowski dealt with in his earliest field work were relatively static.[1] Therefore functionalism is particularly relevant in explaining how such groups continue to reproduce themselves with only minimal changes over many generations. But even Melanesian society, by its complexity and integrative character, attests to a complex history of past innovations. It is impossible to accept, even on the authority of the myths and sagas, that any culture has arisen fully fashioned from the prescriptions of a culture hero or a God. The problem of cultural change can be dealt with only in terms of causal determinations: this is the only basis for the endeavour to understand social reality.

In considering the problem of social change in the light of functionalism we must begin by pointing out that the theory is neither exclusive, nor eclectic. In addition to the principle of function it recognizes two others: *evolution* and *diffusion*. These are basic processes which functionalism attempts to combine into a unique synthesis.[2] With regard to evolution: Malinowski accepts the concept of origins and development as basic to an understanding of cultural change. He maintains that no invention, no revolution, no social or intellectual change, no new institution nor system of belief ever occurs except to satisfy new needs. In other words, there is a continuous process of adaptation by which culture meets the emerging needs of the individual and of the group. Cultural innovations are sifted through the sieve of selection. Only those survive which are fittest to meet the specific needs of the cultural situation. New elements are assimilated and *worked over* by the culture until they fit the on-going system. Culture is an integral whole,[3] a *Gestalt* if you will, continuously changing to accord with the changing needs of the group and of the changing natural environment. The

[1] Malinowski, B. (1937) and his other works on Melanesian society.
[2] Malinowski, B. (1960), pp. 17 ff., 24, 213–14.
[3] Ibid., p. 150. Malinowski, B. (1945), pp. 14, 19, 26, 31, 74, etc. Malinowski, B., cf. (1960), pp. 41, 215, 218.

new idea, religious revelation, artefact, device or moral principle must be organized before it can have any social or cultural relevance. This means that it must be taken over as part of a dynamic system, it must become overtly the possession of a particular social group, affecting its behaviour, before it can be considered a real addition to culture. This is the other aspect of selection: the new thing must receive social approval. This is only to reiterate that the cultural innovation must satisfy a felt need: it is only on this basis that it can achieve objective life and reality.

The concept of diffusion is also basic. This process is defined as the borrowing from another culture of various devices, implements, institutions or beliefs. In the final analysis no distinction between evolution and diffusion is possible. Elements diffuse from one culture to another on the basis that they satisfy needs and ensure survival. Diffusion operates on the basis of contact between cultures: but such contact is not a single act of 'borrowing'. It is an integral *process* to which the analytical categories of functionalism must be applied.[1] It is clear to the functionalist that diffusion and evolution are closely coincident: both are concerned with origins. In the first case attention is concentrated on origins arising from contact with another culture, in the second on origins by invention. Unfortunately, Malinowski does not dwell on the second process; he confines his analysis to the case of culture contact and merely records that cultural innovations can arise through spontaneous initiative or through a process of growth. This is, in fact, the evolutionary aspect of innovation. In culture contact we have a more complex process in which some institutions persist more or less unchanged, others are modified, and there is a gradual evolution of new institutions.

Evolution and diffusion are based on that certain plasticity which is inherent in human nature.[2] This plasticity is the basis of new needs. It gives rise at once to 'spontaneous' development and also to cultural borrowings. The contact situation, where two cultures are physically juxtaposed and intermingle, will itself give rise to new needs. To satisfy these two kinds of new need, new institutions arise, old ones are modified. But culture-contact is not an indiscriminate process of give-and-take. It is

[1] Malinowski, B. (1945), p. vii.   [2] Ibid., p. 8.

directed by definite forces and pressures; these are countered by certain forces of cultural inertia which spring from the system as a whole.[1]

Malinowski describes the sequence of change as follows.[2] There are three phases of culture contact. First of all, we have a reservoir of indigenous customs, beliefs, institutions. This culture complex is relatively stationary, passive, in stable equilibrium. Impinging on it we have a second, active, probably predatory, certainly intrusive, culture. This second culture has its own characteristic interests, intentions, institutions. Thirdly there is the process of contact and change. This may take any of three forms: conflict, cooperation, compromise. As a result changes occur which affect both the indigenous and the intrusive cultures.

The units of transformation are *institutions*.[3] These assume new forms and functions as new needs arise in the contact situation. The whole process conforms to scientific law. We are dealing with a system consisting, we might say, of two complex bodies. This system is disturbed from an original condition of equilibrium. Certain adjustments take place within the system in the direction of achieving a new optimal level of satisfaction of needs. The system then settles back into a new condition of equilibrium.[4] Changes which take place within the system are in terms of the modification, the abolition, the recrudescence of institutions. These constitute the units of the system. The final outcome is a new integral which is neither a simple mixture of elements, nor yet a mere juxtaposition of partially fused elements. A new integral need develops in the culture-contact situation; a new integral institution develops to satisfy it. The new institution operates in terms of a newly-defined function.

Malinowski differs from the classical diffusionists Ratzel, Graebner, Schmidt and others. He emphasizes not the migration of 'traits' or 'trait-complexes' which travel and become embedded as alien enclaves in an unchanged groundmass. His picture is rather of a dynamic process of interchange between a migrating structured figure penetrating a structured groundmass. From this conjunction a new structure, a unity, a *Gestalt*

---

[1] Ibid., p. 19.
[2] Ibid., p. 19, pp. 15 ff., 26, 27, 74.
[3] Ibid., p. vii.
[4] Ibid., p. 27.

is produced. This is true even of material artefacts. They acquire a new 'aura' and certainly a new function within the recipient culture. The bustle and ostrich feathers of the chorus-girl may be physically indistinguishable from the plumes of the African tribal dancer and the posterioral appearance of his steatopygous spouse. But her dance has a different significance, and the ritualized setting in which it takes place (it may be for example, business tycoons engaged in 'conspicuous consumption') fulfils a very different function in the metropolitan compared with the kraal environment.

For these reasons functionalism eschews the study of the isolated details of culture. It declares that analysis must retain the reality of a functioning system. Otherwise a distortion is introduced which stultifies theory and disorients practice. It is the difference between anatomy and physiology, between statics and dynamics. The process of cultural 'borrowing' is very like that of digestion: the bolus of food is broken down and transformed into materials which are then incorporated in new structures.

As Malinowski says:

'Culture change is (not) a static product . . . (not) a system of temporary integration or of harmonized unity . . . (not) a mechanical mixture . . . The phenomena of change are new cultural realities . . .'[1]

It is in such terms as these that functionalism pictures social change.

[1] Malinowski, B. (1945), p. 26.

3
PSYCHOANALYSIS: PERSONALITY STRUCTURE, POLITICS, SOCIAL CHANGE

Arising from the fact that his method of analysing neurotics ('free-association') imposed its own demand that patients' dreams should be analysed, Sigmund Freud was forced to take a professional interest in the creative processes. To begin with, his interest arose from the dream images: he had to devise a method of interpreting these according to some standard procedure.[1] This involved an understanding of the different 'mechanisms' by which the raw materials of everyday life are converted into a more or less coherent pattern (the manifest dream content). The creative process, especially in painting, sculpture and the other visual arts, in literature, as well as in jokes, was discovered by him to be closely related to creativity in dreams.[2] Due to his highly-developed tendency to consider every question in a universal context, he had very quickly come to consider creativity as a general problem.[3] He was interested in how this function might be related to the unconscious processes which he claimed to find underlying neurotic symptoms.

At the most general level, Freud understood *all* human behaviour to stem from unconscious conflicts.[4] He believed that the roots of conflict could be discovered in earliest infancy. In fact, conflict springs originally from the unconscious impulses of aggression and love between the infant and his parents. According to Freud, the strength of the Oedipus conflict, and the way it is resolved, represent the most powerful and determining sources of adult personality.[5] From moment to moment behaviour in the child and in the adult is directed by strong, unconscious compulsions which arise from Oedipus needs and

---

[1] Freud, S. (1900), *Die Traumdeutung*, 1953 ed., Chapter 2.

[2] Ibid., Chapters 5 and 6.

[3] Freud, S. (1905, 1908, 1910, 1914); cf. Getzels, J. W. and Jackson, P. W. (1962), pp. 88–93.

[4] Raeff, P. (1959), pp. 56–64.

[5] McLeish, J. (1963), Chapter 11 for a criticism of this view.

wishes. These unconscious urges are directed, or inhibited, or transformed, through the medium of environmental agencies.

The same principles apply equally to artistic and creative behaviour as to common, everyday behaviour. Artistic behaviour demands an explanation in exactly the same terms and according to the same principles as all other kinds of human activity. For psychoanalysis, it is immaterial that society distinguishes between neurotic, criminal, 'normal', or other kinds of behaviour. In terms of origins and determining tendencies, fundamentally, there is no distinction. Freud says: 'the forces motivating the artist are the same conflicts which drive other people into neurosis'.[1] The way in which the onlooker classifies the outcome of these conflicts, as 'creative' or 'neurotic', depends on how the unconscious has solved the problem of the ever-increasing psychical tension generated by the instincts. So far as the type of mental process and the actual significance of the outcome in the psychic life of the individual are concerned, artistic creation is on exactly the same footing as the creation of symptoms. Both artistic and neurotic creations are *defensive* in function.[2] The pent-up emotional energy of the Oedipus impulses is drained away equally effectively by the symptom as by the artistic creation. Art and neurosis both deny the claims of reality: both represent the triumph of the 'pleasure principle'. The essential difference between them is that neurosis is regressive and destructive in tendency whereas the art-work is progressive and constructive. The illness, although it serves an essential defensive purpose, does not permit the full potentiality of the patient to be realized. The neurosis is crippling. In a sense it is self-destroying as far as the patient is concerned. On the other hand, tension-reduction through artistic creation is in the line of progress. Creation in an external medium releases energy at all levels in the psyche: inner barriers are broken down and a basis is laid for future development of the psyche.[3]

Freud also believed that there was an evolutionary relationship between childhood play, day-dreaming and creativity. This relationship is accounted for by his view that the Oedipus conflicts find expression through each of these activities, which

[1] Freud, S., *Collected Papers*, vol. 4, pp. 178–80.
[2] Ibid., vol. 1, pp. 59–75.
[3] Ibid., vol. 4, pp. 181–2.

serve to reduce the tensions generated by these conflicts. These relations are also vouched for by the fact that the manifest content of the art product, that is, what the product seems to be 'about', refers covertly to the experiences and repressed wishes of childhood.

According to psychoanalytic theory, neurotic symptoms are 'over-determined'. That is to say, current conflicts overlie earlier traumatic experiences in a continuous sequence which stretches back to earliest childhood. So, in precisely the same way, the art product is not only a response to current experience: it catches up resonances of earlier experiences, including especially those of childhood. Like day-dreaming, imaginative creation is a continuation of the play of childhood. Like play, it is cathartic. It serves to release emotions which, when pent-up over a long period, cause damage, perhaps neurosis. The artist's spontaneity is modelled on the unreflective life of the child. The psychic energy essential for creation is generated in the unconscious. The conscious artistic intention is momentarily in harmony with certain repressed impulses. These are released through a particular channel (the art product) in exactly the same way as repressed wishes are expressed by children in play and by the adult in the dream. In art as in dreaming, the censor is off guard because the Oedipal wishes (destructive, incestuous, cannibalistic, obscene) have managed to assume a satisfactory disguise. As the endopsychic censorship is deceived during sleep by the transformation of the latent content into dream symbols,[1] so the symbolism of art enables similar impulses to escape undetected into the public domain.

It is by virtue of a particular conjunction, what Freud calls a 'syntonicity of unconscious and ego' that the two fall so to speak into line for the artist.[2] This syntonicity (a *harmony of intent* would be another way to describe it, except that this implies an element of conscious deliberation foreign to this theory) makes possible special, perfect, creative achievements. The unconscious is able to impose its repressed impulses in an overpowering way on the ego which normally is repelled by them: it is empowered to sweep all opposition away since it has, for the nonce, the support, instead of the active opposition, of

[1] Freud, S., *Die Traumdeutung* (1953 edit.), pp. 310–38, 339–404.
[2] Freud, S., *Collected Papers*, vol. 4, p. 121.

the ego. The normal process in our psychic life is the repression by the ego of 'freely rising', 'spontaneous' ideas. Criticism, which is only one of a great number of repressive mechanisms available to the ego to defend itself against the unconscious, normally strangles the idea at birth. Or it may force the idea to assume a disguise such as prevents its free association with other, related ideas. These related ideas are thus inhibited; they fail to find expression. Creativity is stifled. The intellect constrains the imagination to the point where sterility sets in. Freud quotes Schiller in support of this idea:

'In the case of a creative mind, it seems to me, it is as if the intellect has withdrawn its watchers from the gates: ideas rush in pell-mell, and only then does it review and inspect the multitude. You worthy critics, or whatever you may call yourselves, are ashamed or afraid of the momentary and passing madness found in all real creators. It is the longer or shorter duration of this condition which distinguishes the thinking artist from the dreamer. Hence your complaints of unfruitfulness: you reject too soon and discriminate too severely.'[1]

Freud believes that the investigatory impulse is connected with childhood curiosity, especially about sexual matters. This kind of curiosity develops at a very early age; in most cases by about the third year. Sexual curiosity is connected very closely by psychoanalytic theory with the child's anxiety about the real relations that exist between mother and father. However, all the forces of repression are mobilized against this childhood interest, as indeed they are against any spontaneous expression of sexuality during infancy. Three possibilities open up as outcomes of this nursery battle between the forces of nature and the agents of civilization. First, sexual curiosity may encounter the same fate as happens to certain other manifestations of sexuality in childhood. It undergoes extinction.[2] If this is the outcome, and the extinction is total, the free activity of the individual will be narrowed for life, in that both sexual feeling and originality will be completely extinguished. This consummation, which occurs fairly frequently, generally results from a combination of a powerful individual mechanism of repression, coupled with

[1] F. Schiller writing to Körner on 1 xii 1788 quoted, Freud, S., *Interpretation of Dreams.*

[2] Freud, S., *Essays on Sexuality* (1953), vol. 4, p. 103.

narrow parental, educational and religious prohibitions. In the second possibility, the intellectual development of the individual is sufficiently advanced to withstand the repressive forces. But these cannot be overcome entirely, although in this case the psyche manages to elude the worst results of their stranglehold. The investigatory impulse is forced to lie low, so to speak, until a favourable conjunction of forces permits it to be expressed. But this mode of expression will normally take the form of compulsive reasoning. The creativity of the individual remains at a relatively low ebb. The impulse towards innovation is crippled, it is not extinguished completely. The spontaneous impulses which remain need to ally themselves with the critical and analytical intellect to survive at all. But this union of intellect and spontaneity is hardly viable: it is spontaneity which must be sacrificed. The third case produces the most perfectly developed result from the point of view of artistic achievement. In this case, the energy which is by Nature associated with infantile sexual curiosity is transformed. This energy (otherwise known as *libido*) loses its sexual character by the process of sublimation. In other words, libido is completely detached from its origins and becomes transformed into curiosity. The infantile sexual investigatory impulse being 'purified' of erotic elements, repression is no longer necessary. The total energy (*cathexis*) which was once available to *libidinal curiosity* is now placed, without reservation or inhibition, at the disposal of the artistic or other creative impulse. The creative impulse therefore loses that compulsive, neurotic character which was found to be associated with the second case, since it is now completely freed from the restraining influences of repression. Creativity rises to a new level, high above that of infantile sexuality: it appears as an almost super-human originality and spontaneity.[1]

This is a summary statement of Freud's view of creative activity. It is a necessary basis for understanding the psychoanalytic theory of the origins of historical change.[2] The most elaborate treatment of this question is that of G. R. Taylor. His views are the most comprehensive and coherent explanation of social process given by exponents of this theory. They are most rewarding to consider, being grounded in empirical data and

---

[1] Freud, S., *Leonardo da Vinci*, pp. 46–50.
[2] Taylor, G. R., *The Angel Makers* (1958), cf. also *Sex in History* (1954).

accepting the discipline of method and of fact. Taylor's theory of social change seeks to make up for the shortcomings which many psychologists are conscious of in the historian's approach to history. These are: the naïve character of the psychological assumptions on the basis of which motivations are attributed to historical personages; the unreflecting dependence of the historian on the prejudices and value-judgements of his particular epoch and group; the relative incoherence and self-contradictory character of the explanations of historical tendencies and movements; the lack of psychological definition in the characterization of individuals and historical trends; the contradictions in explanations of analogous or opposed events; the failure really to *explain* any of the alleged associations between personality and events.[1] But criticism of the historian is merely incidental to Taylor's main task. This he conceives to be to supply those psychological concepts and explanations which are needed to overcome weaknesses in the prevailing explanations of social change.

It must be made clear that in providing these concepts Taylor moves entirely within the psychoanalytic universe of discourse. He does not consider other kinds of psychological explanation. His major intent is to establish links between psychiatry and history. But it must also be said that Taylor's use of intuition differs from Freud's. It is a disciplined and sophisticated intuition which takes pleasure in processing the grime and dust of empirical fact embedded in historical records, diaries, journals, periodicals and books of the period. Taylor, unlike Freud, attempts to establish *actual* historical links, instead of substituting analogical trains of thought and psychological interpretations based on more or less free associations.[2] The basic constructs used in explaining change are certainly taken from the windy, though occasionally eloquent, school of Central European Freudian dogmatism. But the voice is that of English empiricism.

The starting point for the investigation of social change is the theory of parental identifications.[3] According to psychoanalytic theory, the child, even at the mother's breast, manifests sexual

---

[1] Taylor, G. R., *The Angel Maker* (1958), p. 342.

[2] Cf. McLeish, J. (1963), Chapter 11.

[3] Taylor, G. R. (1954) and (1958), pp. 148, 171–7, 200–5, 258–9, etc.

feeling. This period of development is in fact the first or *oral* stage of sexuality.[1] The child is unaware that he is an object, distinct from other objects in the universe.[2] His unconscious mentation operates to persuade him that by oral sucking he assimilates the mother to himself. In two ways therefore, by sexuality and cannibalism, he *identifies* with the mother.[3] Identification is the earliest emotional tie with the outside world. But this emotional tie is not an object-love as we understand it. Identification is a peculiar kind of self-love which does not recognize any ego-boundary separating us from the rest of the universe. In the ways in which it expresses itself identification cannot readily be distinguished from object-love. But, in reality, in its origins, the infant's love for the mother is narcissistic in character.

The process of identification is distinguished only with great subtlety from a second kind of defence-mechanism which is called *introjection*. Along with material milk, the infant assimilates certain psychological characteristics of the mother. This is the process of introjection: it is bound up with the desire to have, to retain, and to incorporate the material object which the child fears is in danger of being lost. Identification is an expression of the desire to *become* the object: introjection, on the other hand, represents an unconscious attempt to transform the object into oneself by *digesting* it. The mother-identifier, in the usual case, shows all the characteristics which are associated with a loving mother. The twin processes of identification and introjection work to produce a softness, a concern for welfare, an expressiveness and spontaneous emotionality in the growing child.

At a later stage, the child encounters his father as an object of special interest. On the basis of their common feeling for the mother, and of the care which the father takes of him (similar to, and substitutive of, the care which his mother has shown in the past) the child identifies with the father. This expresses itself in the form of an unconscious wish to be like him, to grow up like him, to take his place in many ways. According to Freudian theory, identification with the father becomes focused

---

[1] Healy, W. and Bronner, A. F. (1949), p. 110.
[2] Freud, S., *Three Essays on Sexuality*, 1953 edit., pp. 171–206.
[3] Healy, W. and Bronner, A. F. (1949), p. 81.

on the specific desire to take his place sexually with the mother. This is the origin of the Oedipus complex.

The incestuous wish introduces a hostile element into the relationship between father and child. Consciously or unconsciously, they become hostile rivals. Death-wishes and all kinds of aggressive impulses are directed or openly expressed by the child towards his father. The child's psychic life becomes complicated by ambivalent emotions which include love-hate attitudes directed not only towards the father, but also to the mother.[1]

With accepting and loving parents and during the process of growing up, the destructive impulses of the Oedipus complex are redirected towards creative outlets. Most children will naturally introject elements from both parents: the destructive impulses will be 'civilized' by more amiable components accepted from both parents. The majority of people will develop to adulthood as some sort of 'balanced' personality, as far as parental and maternal characteristics are concerned. But extreme kinds of development are possible. These are based on physical constitution in part, on child-rearing practices in part, and on the abnormal qualities of particular parents in part.

Two cases are considered by Taylor as being of special significance. In the first case, a variety of incidents and attitudes generate the unconscious conviction that the mother is an unloving betrayer. For example, a very sharp weaning may be followed by an extremely strict toilet-training. Harsh punishment of the child may be accompanied by a marked and freely expressed preference for the father's love. The relationship of identification may, as a consequence, become sharply transformed into its polar opposite, rejection. A love, which in any case is by its very nature ambivalent, becomes transformed into a rooted hatred. This finds expression in many different kinds of overt and unconscious attitudes and behaviour. For one thing, identification is now entirely with the father. In Taylor's terminology (adapted from Flugel) *patrism* becomes the dominant unconscious tendency. This basic tendency expresses itself in a great variety of attitudes and practices. Typically, the patrist or father-identifier (who may be of either sex) is strongly

[1] Freud, S., *Complete Works*, Standard edit., vol. 11, 1957, pp. 46–8; ibid., vol. 19, 1961, pp. 31–9, 48–9.

committed to an authoritarian régime of discipline. Women are considered by the patrist to be constitutionally inferior. They are the 'weaker sex': this really means that great care must be taken of their virtue and chastity. The patrist, in his or her behaviour and speech, acts on the belief that the influence of women has to be systematically weakened by legal enactment, by giving them an inferior or no education at all, by all manner of social conventions, forms and styles, such as art, dress, religion, manners.[1] Under a patrist régime, all of these combine to point the inferiority of women to men.

On the other hand, the child may perceive his father not as a model but as an unwanted interloper. The mother is regarded as the source of tender feeling, of care for the child's interests against a hated father, of comfort in a relatively hostile psychological environment. These attitudes lead to the process of exclusive mother-identification or *matrism*. Mother-identification develops on the basis of a free nursery régime which embodies slow and lenient weaning, relaxed toilet-training, a non-restrictive upbringing and a readiness by the mother to enter into the child's world of play and fantasy.[1] The matrist therefore tends to place a great emphasis on *welfare* and hardly any on *property*. He considers pleasure, not duty, to be the prime aim of life. He values happiness; he works for the equality of women, and for numerous social causes which aim to diminish suffering and remove the barriers to human association which society erects.

In working out this theory, Taylor is particularly concerned with the eighteenth century in England (1700–1850). He finds no difficulty in establishing the existence of the extreme kinds of behaviour and of attitudes associated with patrism and matrism. This part of his work consists of rather more than merely giving names to already well-known phenomena. He demonstrates an inner connection between all kinds of attitudes and qualities. These were certainly known to exist before he referred to them, but they were regarded simply as interesting types of eccentricity, not a matter for historical explanation. Taylor has shown, for example, how authoritarianism is closely associated with worship of a father-deity. These are found along with antifeminism and a primitive and restrictive attitude

[1] Taylor, G. R. (1958), pp. 171 ff.

in sexual matters. Patrism expresses itself in coherent attitudes to art, to scientific inquiry, to property. It is preoccupied with notions of very strict punishment for sexual irregularities especially—masturbation and homosexuality being singled out as the most heinous types of misdemeanours.[1]

On the other hand, matrism expresses itself in liberal attitudes in politics, religion and social questions. It is associated with a high regard for Nature, which is often personified as a woman. It is characteristic of matrism that it is found to be normally associated with deference to women. Compared to patrism, historically speaking, it adopts a more understanding attitude to common human weaknesses and manifests a fraternal sympathy for the under-dog. Mother-identifiers tend to be overmuch concerned with incest as a social and personal problem and hardly at all with homosexuality, a central concern of the conservative patrist. Many other social attitudes and personal qualities are linked together in the seminal concepts of matrism and patrism.

Taylor tries to justify the view that social change obeys underlying laws of causation. He recognizes a certain movement in history which is phasal in character. During some phases patrism is dominant. These are followed by periods when matrism is widespread and the dominant trend. In such historical periods we are observing extremes of social development. Matrists and patrists are both unbalanced, not to say neurotic, types. They tend to be so caught up in their Oedipal conflicts that they can make hardly any contribution to social life.[2] However, the mother-identifier tends to be a social innovator, more so than the patrist. This is because the patrist is convinced that any change represents a criticism of the earlier generation of fathers. But neither will the matrist be responsible for large and useful changes. In the most usual case, he will be so involved in the pursuit of pleasure and the gratification of his own ego-needs that he will be wholly unable to devote himself single-mindedly to desirable social changes. It is when society is at a point of balance, consisting of individuals with mixed parental identifications, that the greatest changes, including social achievements, will be made.[2]

[1] Taylor, G. R., *Sex in History*, 1954.
[2] Taylor, G. R. (1958), pp. 234–5, 348, 353.

The theory of parental identifications is but a small part of the story. Matrism-patrism represents the first great dichotomy which enables us to distinguish between individuals of different type. This classification carries with it the maximum amount of individual variation in social, religious, artistic and behavioural aspects. As has been said, matrism and patrism are polar extremes; the majority of people are in the middle range, exhibiting mixed parent-identifications. Having classified individuals as matrists and patrists, a great deal remains to be said before we have any detailed picture of them as real persons.[1] Taylor is interested in types, but he is interested too in the unique qualities of particular individuals. The puritan, the romantic, the classicist, the libertine, the quaker and others loom large in his pages. He goes further than a mere typology in trying to understand the peculiar qualities of such individuals as John Howard, Hannah More, Lord Byron, Shaftesbury, and many others. Generally he chooses representative individuals for study, that is, those who have influenced large groups.

The method of choice which he uses in attempting to explain various types and individuals is to relate their specific personality structures to early upbringing and childhood experiences.[2] The main problem of this period in history, the eighteenth and early nineteenth centuries, is to explain how the attitudes and standards of the trading middle classes came to be accepted by the ruling class. Taylor is, above all, concerned with explaining the origin of Puritan attitudes and sentiments and the manner in which these became accepted as the dominant social mores. He regards these attitudes and sentiments as arising out of nursery experience. The questions he raises have to do with the (Puritan) obsession with guilt, their preoccupation with death, their severe morality, and the narrowly-circumscribed quality of their emotional and volitional life. The key to this specific constellation of traits Taylor finds in a variety of nursery practices widespread in this group: allowing children 'to cry themselves out'—a practice general in the eighteenth century; the harmful swaddling of infants in tight bands restricting all movement; the overwhelming stress laid by parents on the allegedly harmful consequences of masturbation; the severe toilet training practised by these

---

[1] Taylor, G. R., (1958), pp. 204 ff.   [2] Ibid., pp. 310, 323-33.

parents and their general emphasis on personal cleanliness; the early and abrupt weaning characteristic of this group; the proscription of any show of maternal affection; the oral frustrations resulting from a peculiar combination of early weaning and overfeeding; the extraordinary demands made on the child of tender years with regard to rote-learning; the collateral emphasis on sermons, prayers, repentance, death; lastly, the extreme punishments which were meted out from earliest childhood, associated usually with the inducement of irrational terror of supernatural retributions. These methods of child-rearing are illustrated in authenticated detail from biographical material. Taylor concludes:

'It will be seen that the various factors act so as to reinforce one another. The genital taboos probably help to create the anal fixation. The anal insistence on restraint motivates the use of swaddling bands; these contribute to the fund of aggression. The aggression strengthens the death-wishes, and these strengthen the guilt. The guilt in turn ensures the transmission of the genital taboos, and so the circle is completed. Other links will suggest themselves: thus the emotional impairment resulting from aphanisis* is what enables the parent to be so severe, while the various frustrations create the situation in which aphanisis can be evoked. It is striking, for instance, how the Puritan group not only practised just those actions, such as letting the child cry itself out, most calculated to produce the desired effect, but also attacked precisely those actions of the upper class, such as farming children out, which were most likely to create the opposite effect. This is no accident. For instance, it is just because the Puritan values restraint that he employs swaddling bands, and it is because he is emotionally inhibited that he can, unmoved, watch a child cry itself into exhaustion, where a more responsive person would feel driven to intervene. Conversely, an over-sensitive person would intervene too readily and thus "spoil" the child.'[1]

This description illustrates a circular chain of causes and effects which, unchecked, could result in melancholia and

---

* *Aphanisis* (Ernest Jones) is a condition of emotional exhaustion produced in children allowed to 'cry themselves out'. According to this author it is associated with a permanent incapacity to feel emotion at all.

[1] Taylor, G. R. (1958), p. 333.

suicide. Indeed, these were extremely common phenomena in England under this mode of upbringing. The chain could be broken in other ways than suicide or mental illness. Full-blown insanity aside (typically, schizophrenia or religious mania), 'conversion'[1] was a common way of beginning a new life. Conversion as a psychological device was associated historically with the Methodists and Evangelical Christians, active during this period. The psychological significance of conversion lies in the absolute conviction that Christ died for the *personal salvation* of the newly 'awakened' individual. It was preceded very commonly, as in Hannah More's case, with the death of the father or some close relative. Normally it followed on a lifetime of oppression by an overpowering sense of guilt, of depression, and fear of an outraged God. The experience was accompanied, perhaps it entirely consisted of, a tremendous lightening of the spirits, a relief from the fear of death and of eternal punishment, coupled with a joyful expectation of attaining everlasting life. It seems probable, following Taylor, and in the light of Kinsey's research, that the overpowering conviction of personal damnation and oppression of the spirit characteristic of this group were both based on masturbation guilt.[2] The nature of the literature about the alleged physical, mental and spiritual effects of this practice, coupled with the methods undoubtedly used by parents to put a stop to this kind of self-indulgence by children[3] would almost certainly produce a great number of compulsive masturbators, obsessed with the burden of sin and the fear of death, but unable to desist. The vicious circle: compulsive masturbation, producing strong guilt feelings, which reinforce the compulsion to masturbate could be broken at its strongest link by religious conversion. The burden of guilt was lifted, a new hope was born which made possible a reformation in this sexual behaviour.

The basic question which Taylor sets out to answer, and which has been referred to above, is one of the central historical problems of the eighteenth and nineteenth century. It is this: how did the trading middle classes succeed in imposing their ideas of moral behaviour, of manners, and religion on the rest

---

[1] Ibid., pp. 104 ff.   [2] Ibid., pp. 326-7.

[3] Ellis, A. and Abarnel, A. (edits.), *Encyclopaedia of Sexual Behaviour*, vol. I, pp. 188, 204-15; Kinsey, *et altera*, 1948.

of society? In his search for materials bearing on this question Taylor discovered that the historical record gives *no* support to the traditional view of eighteenth and nineteenth century moralities.[1] The change from matrist to patrist attitudes occurred much earlier (1790–1800) than is commonly believed, and was not at all associated with the views and practices of the monarchy. In fact, Taylor proposes the theory that the impetus of the moralists was beginning to fade *even before* Victoria became Queen.[2] The problem remains in that a social change did take place. But the victory of middle-class ideas was neither so complete as is generally believed, nor did it take place at the time traditionally assigned. The lower classes remained almost entirely unaffected by the moral, religious and social ideas of the middle classes. The upper classes had very little genuine religious conviction even at the end of the period; it is true that, for various reasons, certain members pretended to beliefs and practices, none of which they experienced with any inwardness.

The well-known fact remains that the middle-class religion of the period was commonly associated with the 'commercial virtues': thrift, conscientiousness in the daily task, placing a high value on the use of time, and so on. The traits of orderliness, obstinacy, parsimony, and an obsession with bodily cleanliness, have been singled out by Freud as belonging to the so-called 'anal' character.[3] The interest in money, characteristic of this group, belongs to this same basic personality structure. Anal love expresses itself in the form of bestowing material gifts rather than by an expression of tenderness. This is because the anal personality is severely restricted in powers of feeling and expressing emotion. Thus, generalized love or a positive feeling directed towards social groups is expressed by this character type in the form of philanthropy, benefactions, patronage. The feelings are hardly at all engaged. The philanthropist need not enter into the *actual* needs of the recipients of his charity: indeed, the philanthropist often expresses in private his strong aversion to the object of his benefactions. The anal constellation of traits is suffused by a general attitude of possessiveness and proprietorship which is of the essence of this personality structure. The hate, frustration and aggression associated with the

[1] Taylor, G. R. (1958), pp. 83–6.   [2] Ibid., p. 104.
[3] Freud, S. (1908), *Collected Papers*, 1949 edit., pp. 45–50.

42

Oedipus complex here attains an especially high level of development. Sadism is a common manifestation at the anal level of sexuality.[1]

The source of the anal personality, if we follow the psychoanalytic view, lies in the nursery. In the normal process of growth the child passes first through the oral stage. In the second stage certain pleasures and frustrations continue to be associated with the mouth region, but the anus asserts its supremacy as an erogenous zone. It takes over from the mouth as the prime centre of pleasure and of frustration. The lifeforce or libido, which previously expressed itself in the form of oral sexuality, now manifests itself through the excretory functions. The strict bowel-training and obsession with bodily cleanliness which is associated with Puritan upbringing may result in fixation of the libido at the anal level. The absolute inhibition by the Puritan parents of any expression of genital sexuality (the next stage of normal child development) has a similar effect in binding or fixating the energy available. The libido is bound at the anal level: it is not allowed to progress naturally and spontaneously to the genital level. The main point being established in this argument is that there is a coherent pattern which links together certain leading qualities of the Puritan personality, and that this coherence is not accidental.[2] In particular, the specialized 'commercial virtues' can best be understood as belonging to a constellation of traits generated by early conditioning at the infantile level.[3] Education merely puts the capstone on a structure which is completed even before the child learns to read, long before any social influence other than the family can possibly work on him.

Given this particular pattern or constellation of traits (interest in money, industriousness, reliability) it is clear that economic power and, as a direct consequence, political power will fall inevitably into the hands of the middle classes. Those individuals, belonging to the lower classes, who happen to have the same outlook and personality structure will be upwardly mobile. They will tend to rise socially and become members of the middle classes. The upper classes too will gradually take on

[1] Ibid., Freud, S. (1905), pp. 173–243.
[2] Taylor, G. R. (1958), pp. 148, 329.   [3] Ibid., pp. 161–5.

an appearance of middle-class virtue as the new rulers assert their social hegemony.[1] Some upper-class members will actually be converted to the patrist morality and religion, and will bring up their children in the new way. Psychoanalysts would probably concede that, at a crude level of analysis, we can interpret social and historical changes in terms of economic factors. But, according to Taylor's assumptions, the spirit of capitalism and the ethos of Puritanism are both effects which arise from a common cause. The association between capitalism and protestantism made much of by Weber, Troeltsch, and Tawney is not a cause-and-effect relationship. Neither is it a natural or inevitable conjunction. The fact is that the 'commercial virtues' are not derived from Christianity: they arise *in spite of* the clearest directives against them in the New Testament. It is the anal elements in the Puritan personality which constitute the real source of the 'commercial virtues',[2] and which account for the moralizing character of this group (this has no real connection with religion as such). The intensity with which these pseudo-religious characteristics express themselves in the Puritan personality is due to the strength of identification with the father figure. The two kinds of apparent causal factor, father-identification and anal fixation, are to be accounted for by the nursery training of the infant Puritan. The patrist morality became dominant in the eighteenth century as a direct consequence of the commercial success of the trading-middle-classes: historically, they were bearers of the 'message'. This, briefly, is Taylor's answer to the historical problem posed above.[3]

The anal personality manifests a remarkable fascination with words: this springs in part from the obsessional elements in this personality structure. The orderliness, which is a leading and defining trait of the anal character, extends to verbal matters as to everything else. One of the most striking features of the Puritan is the extraordinary significance he attaches to the written and spoken word.[4] Religion, for him, is a matter of an inspired book, the reading of which in some mysterious, magical fashion makes for salvation. Bible fundamentalism is the characteristic form of Puritan religion. The genealogy of Moses

---

[1] Taylor, G. R. (1958), pp. 334–6.   [2] Ibid., pp. 96, 161, 164.
[3] Ibid., pp. 338–57.   [4] Ibid., p. 148.

carries the same significance for salvation as the Sermon on the Mount. In terms of edification, a sermon (once actually delivered) on the biblical text 'Therefore' has the same value as one on the text 'Love one another'. Sermons have a peculiar attraction for the anal patrist. It is not enough to listen to two or three lengthy sermons on Sunday. These must be supplemented by 'family readings' of printed sermons. Family prayers are also a normal, indeed the most important part, of everyday life. The religious man is 'instant in prayer' at every moment of the day. In training the child, precept and *not* example is regarded as the most effective method. Conversely, a sinister and magical quality is attributed to statements against religion.[1] Blasphemy is singled out as a peculiarly horrible crime, deserving instant retaliation by God, failing this, condign punishment by the state. The crime of blasphemy is extended to cover a great number of cases, many of which have no direct reference to the name of God at all. Novel-reading is also condemned. This is so even when (as in Hannah More's *Coelebs in search of a Wife*) the novel is consciously designed to inculcate virtue and religious truth.[2] Plays and play-reading, poetry, secular tracts—all are under the same total ban. The vocabulary of everyday speech must be constantly purified of words which could possibly carry any sexual or physical meaning. Euphemisms or foreign words for bodily functions are permissible only up to the point when, by common usage, their meaning has become so widely-known that they partake of the original sinfulness of the Anglo-Saxon equivalents.

According to Taylor, the Puritan finds his polar opposite exemplified in the Romantics of the late eighteenth and early nineteenth centuries. The contrast can be illustrated in a table:[3]

Puritan, patrist type	*Romantic, matrist type*
1. Believes in the inherent wickedness of man.	Believes evil is in environment.
2. Believes in a remote God.	A beneficent and concerned God.
3. Inhibited in speech and behaviour.	Spontaneous, uninhibited.

[1] Cf. Freud, S. on 'Animism, magic and the omnipotence of thought'—Chapter 3 of *Totem and Tabu*.

[2] Taylor, G. R. (1958), pp. 171-7. [3] Ibid., pp. 171-7.

Puritan, patrist type	Romantic, matrist type
4. Autocratic disciplinarian, with a sense of personal isolation.	Democratic in attitudes, having a sense of kinship with others.
5. Believes in the subjection of women.	Pro-feminist, for equality of the sexes.
6. Distrusts science and popular education.	Supports science and popular education.
7. Preoccupied with homosexual themes.	Preoccupied with incest themes.
8. Disbelieves in the possibility of progress.	Has Arcadian and Utopian tendencies.
9. Has a certain horror of nature.	Expresses a deep love of nature.
10. Has a dislike for children and animals, based on theory of natural depravity.	Likes children and emphasizes the goodness and spontaneity of the child.

The fact that some leading English romantics became conservative (patrists) in middle age in their social attitudes does not escape Taylor's notice. He explains this change by citing two processes. First, there is the normal process of change, the basis for which he leaves undefined. Secondly, he recognizes another dichotomous trait which gives rise to further possible variations of type. There is a division which separates those with 'thin-walled egos' from those with 'thick-walled egos'.[1] The thin-walled type has great difficulty in dissociating himself from others and from nature: his ego-boundary is relatively indeterminate. The best example is the German romantic E. T. A. Hoffman. Speaking through one of his characters he says: 'My own ego, the sport of a cruel accident, was dissolved into strange forms and floated helplessly away on the sea of circumstances.'[2]

The theme of ego disruption and ego-substitution is very common in Hoffman's works and in those of German writers of the romantic school. It is found also in certain groups in England, not necessarily matrist, as the romantics are. The Cambridge Platonists, of whom Henry More is the most repre-

[1] Taylor, G. R. (1958), 189 ff., 193, 198.
[2] Hoffman, E. T. A. quoted, Taylor, G. R. op. cit., pp. 189-93.

sentative, show this thin-walled ego tendency very clearly, although they were patrists in their moral and social views.[1] The Puritan, on the other hand, manifests an ego with thick, impermeable boundaries. Thus, he finds it difficult to enter into any true communion with others, sympathizing, understanding and influencing them in a human, social context. If we assume that personality can undergo progressive changes through time as a consequence of certain kinds of experience, there is no difficulty in explaining the changes in social attitudes of (say) Wordsworth or Coleridge. According to Taylor these changes arise from progressive thickening of the ego-walls, possibly to the acceptance of patrist views by these writers, with changes in their parental identifications due to advancing years. It is, of course, possible for individuals first to reject and then to accept the father-image. This can happen, for example, in conversion.[2] In fact, the situation is fluid and dynamic so far as parental identifications are concerned. This is a necessary postulate for Taylor. Otherwise it would be difficult to understand how fashions in religion and morality could change at all. If child-rearing practices are handed down from generation to generation, even allowing for intermarriage and social mobility, it is difficult to see how any basic change in social attitudes could come about, unless the psychological scheme is flexible enough to include certain kinds of dynamisms productive of long-term changes.

The concept of ego-boundaries is important in enabling us to understand how it comes about that Puritan and Romantic can approximate to each other in certain aspects of their behaviour. For one thing, both are individualists. But the quality of their individualism expresses itself in different life-patterns. This is explained as follows:

'The thick-walled patrist is an individualist in the sense that he feels a sense of isolation from his fellow men, and is therefore enabled to operate an economic system which is based on the assumption that men are isolated units, responding only to market forces and uninfluenced by sympathies, traditions or irrational impulses. In contrast, the Romantic has a strong feeling of kinship with others, and rejects competitive economic schemes in favour of cooperative ones. But the Romantic is an

[1] Taylor, G. R. (1958), pp. 193–203.   [2] Ibid., p. 199.

individualist in the sense that he admires individual uniqueness, where the patrist wishes all people to conform to an ideal type. We may say that the thick-walled patrist is an economic individualist, but a moral conformist.'[1]

This distinction also clarifies the nature of the philanthropic impulses of the two groups. The Romantic responds in terms of a spontaneous impulse of pity for some actual victim of misfortune. He is interested in discovering and succouring the real needs of the individual present in the here-and-now. It is a weakness in him that he is unable to enter into any large and continuing scheme of benevolence directed at assisting groups who are far away and out of sight. On the other hand, the Puritan considers charity to be a duty imposed on him in terms of an abstract principle. He enters readily into schemes for organized, impersonal charities directed typically towards causes remote from his everyday life. Thus, he may be a strong opponent of slavery abroad, organizing a mass campaign for its abolition, sparing no effort in the task. But at the same time, he remains relatively insensitive to the dire straits of people on his very doorstep, suffering perhaps worse conditions than the black slaves in the West Indies. Or if he is percipient enough to attend to this fact he feels no moral obligation to do anything about it. It is also true that when he *is* at last moved by the condition of an individual near at hand he shows no understanding of the actual need which must be satisfied. Instead of bread he offers a stone—more commonly perhaps, a Bible.[2]

The difference in depth of feeling and involvement with others is also bound up with the inhibition of impulse. It is a central feature of the education of the Puritan that spontaneity and natural impulse are restrained, almost to an absolute degree. As a consequence the Puritan manifests qualities of *literalness* in a very marked degree. This is to be found running through all aspects of the behaviour of the thick-walled, anal, patrist Puritan.[3] For him, Biblical inspiration is not merely a matter of the *sense* of a given passage: it extends to single words,

---

[1] Taylor, G. R. (1958), p. 233.

[2] Ibid., pp. 247–8; William Wilberforce springs to mind in this connection. The contrast between his attitudes to black slavery and wage-slavery has been drawn at length by the Hammonds.

[3] Ibid., pp. 89 ff.

even to commas. The Bible, in particular the Old Testament, contains a complete guide to everything—moral behaviour, religious doctrine, the history of the Jews, scientific knowledge, the problems of everyday life (to which solutions can readily be found by turning up a passage at random), the future life—indeed everything. A pathological absence of imagination and spontaneous feeling results from this kind of education.

The Romantic, on the other hand, cultivates the imagination by every means open to him. Fairy-tales, stories and novels, a vivid use of colour in everyday life, the non-representational principle in art, elaborate dress and manners, the emphasis on 'natural' wildness in landscape gardening, the use of ornament in architecture and interior decoration—these represent only a few ways in which the Romantic imagination is cultivated, even allowed to run riot. Thus the degree of spontaneity or lack of it gives another dimension which must be incorporated in the study of personality and history.[1]

Aggression, sadistic in character, is also common amongst patrists. This is explained by Taylor on the basis of the frustration-aggression hypothesis.[2] The infant, tied tightly in swaddling clothes, sharply weaned when a week old or less, growing up in a restrictive, punitive environment, with his every natural impulse strangled as soon as born, can dispose of some of the tremendous load of frustration and unhappiness generated by these methods through crying. But some large part of the total quantity of frustration is perforce transformed into aggressive impulses. Many of these find overt expression. For instance, this very system of child-rearing itself testifies to sadistic and aggressive impulses in the parents. Presumably they are inflicting some part of the frustrations they themselves suffered in childhood. Personal violence between husband and wife is also common in this century. Corporal punishment and a ritualized savagery practised on the weak and helpless are, in fact, endemic in patrist groups. Concealed forms of aggression flourish[3] beside the more overt.

The matrist system of child-rearing and education on the other hand is permissive and non-violent. The upper classes

---

[1] Ibid., pp. 89 ff., 211 ff.
[2] Dollard, J. *et altera* (1944).
[3] Taylor, G. R. (1958), *passim.*

'spoiled' their children by all sorts of indulgences. Children were never or rarely punished; they were allowed to learn by suffering the consequences of their own actions in accord with Rousseau's principles. The patrist conception, that the first task of education is to 'break the will of the child', was foreign to this system of education. When it demanded expression, aggression was carefully limited by prescribed forms, such as the duel. 'The cut direct' was but one of a great number of formal methods of conveying displeasure, overt aggression being expressed by minimal physical indications.

In this way Taylor unravels the secrets of historical change. Psychological factors are taken to be the necessary cause of social change. Human personality is the variable to which social mechanisms are linked to bring about alterations in the attitudes and habits of groups and in the social system. Thus far, he has used six major personality variables in accounting for change:

(i)   the nature of introjected parental images, whether paternal or maternal;
(ii) the level of fixation of infantile libido, whether oral, anal or genital;
(iii) the character of ego-boundaries, whether thin-walled or thick-walled;
(iv) the degree to which overt aggression is expressed, whether extreme or absent;
(v)   the presence or absence of extreme guilt feelings;
(vi) the spontaneity of response in contrast to extreme inhibition of natural impulse and expressive behaviour.[1]

Theoretically, this classification is capable of generating ninety-six types of personality. If we consider mother-rejectors and father-rejectors to be special types distinct from patrists and matrists respectively, the extended classification generates one hundred and ninety two types as theoretical possibilities. Taylor does not seem to have made this calculation. But he has something to say about the frequency with which particular types occur in the period under investigation.

'There is no theoretical reason why every conceivable combination of these elements should not occur in actual life, and we might therefore expect the various types to appear in

[1] Taylor, G. R. (1958), pp. 200–5.

approximately equal numbers. However, while instances of almost every combination can be found in real life, the striking thing is that, in practice, most of the combinations are rare: sometimes only a single instance can be found. In contrast, one, or perhaps two, combinations appear quite widely. Moreover, the proportions gradually alter. Father-identification is commoner than mother-identification throughout the period, and as the century progresses, guilty and inhibited father-identification becomes still more widespread. Similarly, anal characteristics appear with increasing frequency. It follows that major cultural influences—probably in the field of child environment—must have been at work to produce this result.'[1]

It is of some interest, to take one example, that Taylor was unable to identify any mother-rejectors during this whole period of one hundred and fifty years.[2]

To sum up Taylor's view: he asserts that certain kinds of psychological process are the ultimate explanation of historical phenomena. Personality, built up through child-rearing practices to which each new generation is subjected, are the real motive force of history. In the period under discussion, the historical process consists in the slow diffusion upwards, and to some extent downwards, of manners, beliefs and standards from the trading middle classes. The reason for the acceptance of the mores of the middle classes by society in general lies in their increasing control of the levers of power. This increasing influence and power are a direct result of the advantages which accrue to them by virtue of their possessing (as part of their personality structure) the 'commercial virtues' of industry, single-mindedness and thrift.

[1] Ibid., p. 204. [2] Ibid., pp. 200–5.

4

SOCIAL ACTION AND SOCIAL CHANGE

In the action theory Parsons[1] in large measure follows a well-trodden path. He takes as his starting point the social system. This is clearly made up of institutions which, in turn, are made up of roles. Roles are generated from actions. The social system therefore falls into place as one of several possible action systems, explicable in terms of the general action theory. Social actions are but one of a group of possible types of action. In addition to society there are three other systems which belong under this rubric of action systems. They interpenetrate and interact with each other. These systems are nature, personality, and the culture system. The social system is regarded as being independent of the others. That is to say, *logically* speaking, it is quite distinct although as an empirical fact society is composed of individuals who share a common culture and a common life. We can start with Parsons' definition:

'The social system consists of a plurality of interacting persons motivated in terms of a tendency to the "optimization of gratification" and whose relation to their situations, including each other, is defined and mediated in terms of a system of culturally structured and shared symbols.'[2]

For conceptual analysis, the social system can be distinguished from the cultural and personality systems, and the system of organic nature. Parsons seems to attempt always to visualize systems-problems in terms of empty boxes, the usual number of boxes being four. For example, as we have seen, reality as a whole comes parcelled out in the boxes on p. 53.

These four systems interpenetrate and interact with each other. But for the purpose of analysis they must be kept *logically* separated. It could be because of the fact that nature 'belongs' to the natural scientist, culture to the anthropologist and the

[1] Sources for Parsons' Theories are especially: Parsons, T. and Shils, E. A. (1951); Parsons, T. (1952, 1954, 1960); Parsons, T. and Smelser, N. (1957); Parsons, T. *et altera* (1955, 1961); Black, M. (ed. 1961).
[2] Parsons, T. (1952), pp. 5–6.

personality system to the psychologist. This leaves the social system for the sociologist, an admirable and traditional division of labour.

A system can be defined as a complex of elements in mutual interaction. None of the four boxes containing reality are completely closed. They each admit materials from the outside. For instance, the social system takes part in closely interacting processes with the other three systems, the cultural, organic and personality systems. So it is with each of the systems. They are *open* systems, signifying that each has transactions with its

Society (the social system)	Man (the personality system)
Culture (the cultural system)	Nature (the organic system)

environment, which, of course, consists of the other three systems. Each has an intake from the others and outputs to them.

The four systems also resemble each other in having built-in restorative processes which prevent them from 'running down'. Each *tends* to remain in 'a steady state' in consequence of various homeostatic or self-regulating mechanisms. This means that neither the various exchanges which take place across boundaries, nor any internal changes which take place within the system can seriously disrupt the on-going processes which maintain the normal life of the system. In general, there is a process of differentiation which results in an increase in the complexity of each of the systems with the passing of time. There is also an increase of order within each system (although it is possible that reality as a whole is subject to entropy,[1] that is, a gradual running-down towards extinction).

In the three systems of society, personality and culture we are dealing with *action systems*. The principles embodied in the

[1] Parsons, T. *et altera* (1951). Toward a General Theory of Action, especially Chapter I.

general theory of action apply to each of these systems. The same general processes and variables are to be found in each. For example, each is divided into the same number and type of subsystems. This happens because, to ensure the continuation of the system, exactly the same functional imperatives (or essential constraints) are found in each. To put it otherwise, by its very nature an open system demands that certain conditions be fulfilled if the system is to survive. According to the action theory, these conditions are such that each system requires to have four necessary elements or subsystems. An action system, whether it be nature, culture, personality or society, demands:

(A) an adaptive, instrumental, object-manipulations subsystem; (G) an expressive, consummatory, goal-gratification subsystem; (L) a latent, pattern-maintenance, meaning-integration and energy-regulation subsystem; and (I) an integrative, expressive, sign-manipulation subsystem.

This structure can be illustrated thus:

Adaptive subsystem (A)	Goal-gratification subsystem (G)
Pattern-maintenance subsystem (L)	Integrative subsystem (I)

In the action theory, the problem of method is solved by according sociology the status of a science. The scientific method is as appropriate in studying culture, personality, and society as it is to the study of nature. This is no longer a matter for discussion. Undoubtedly, there are certain peripheral questions which remain to be solved; but the basic question, whether the systematic procedures of science should, and can be used in studying social behaviour must be answered affirmatively. Academic discourse and the intuitive method can generate hypotheses, but must fail to provide agreed solutions.[1] In sociology, the method of analytical abstraction is mandatory,

[1] Cf. McLeish, J., Clinical intuition: a tutorial discussion, *Medical World*, March 1963; cf. Parsons, T. and Smelser, N. (1957), p. 284.

as in the other sciences. Theoretical explanations of the social system must be in terms of concepts and logical propositions which are capable of being verified by some empirical procedure.

It is certainly impossible in such an analysis to encompass the whole of empirical reality. Selection is essential. The scientific scheme must be simple, but not any sort of simplicity will do. Abstraction from reality must proceed according to stated criteria or canons of method. For instance, the analytical scheme must relate to an empirical reality. In that sense it must be a valid explanation of processes and phenomena which proceed 'out there'. In addition, the explanation must be conceptually precise as well. That is, it should be parsimonious of concepts and hypotheses, it must be non-repetitive and non-tautologous.[1]

S_A	S_G
S_L	S_I

The ideal to which science aspires is to generate a system of analytical propositions which are closely related so that they are, in fact, logically interdependent. Although this may not be how they originated in reality, it should be possible to deduce these propositions from a set of primary postulates and definitions. This is the task in which Parsons is engaged, while admitting freely that the scheme provided by the action theory is still far from complete. Earlier generalizations, such as society as an organism, or a mechanism, or a collection of subjective forms, are useless in defining the field. They are *reductionist* in tendency: that is, the subject matter of sociology is conceptualized in terms of some other branch of scientific enquiry, such as biology or physics.

As we have seen, Parsons conceived the social system as an open one interacting in complex ways with the other three systems which surround it. Because of its nature as an *action* system it is differentiated internally to cater for the four functional imperatives: the subsystem goal-gratification S_G, the

[1] McLeish, J., *The Science of Behaviour* (1963), Chapter I.

adaptive subsystem S_A, the integrative subsystem S_I and the pattern-maintenance subsystem S_L (see diagram on p. 55).

These subsystems are themselves open, and have the same characteristics as other open action systems. Interchanges, which are called inputs and outputs, take place across the boundaries of the subsystems. These subsystems are normally in equilibrium, resembling the total system in this respect; each functions in accordance with the principle of homeostatic control. In summary, society can best be defined as a large-scale, self-sufficient and persistent system of social interaction. It falls under the necessity of maintaining a great number of processes and subsystems essential for the survival and well-being of a going concern. To quote:

'Because empirical organization of the system is a fundamental focus, the norm, as it were, must be the conception of an empirically self-subsistent social system. If we add the consideration of duration sufficiently long to transcend the life span of the normal human individual, recruitment by biological reproduction and socialisation of the oncoming generation become essential aspects of such a social system. A social system of this type, which meets all the essential functional prerequisites of long term persistence from within its own resources, will be called a *society*.'[1]

The fundamental units which make up the social system are activities, roles, and collectivities. Activities originate in the fact that human beings pursue particular goals which satisfy specific needs. In the simplest case, ego persuades alter to perform a designated action with him. The response of alter in performing the act forces ego to evaluate their joint activity and to plan future behaviour on the basis of what has been learned. Alter is also forced to evaluate not only ego's overtures but their joint performance. This is done on the basis of the gratifications which accrue to each as a result of the cooperative action. This analysis would appear to be heavily weighted on the cognitive side, but the social act has goal-directed and affective aspects also. It is goal-directed in that it leads, or is intended to lead, to some valued end. It is affective insofar as ego and alter are emotionally involved in its success or failure.[2]

[1] Parsons, T. (1952), p. 19; cf. Parsons, T. (1961), pp. 30–79.
[2] Parsons, T., op. cit., especially 1951, 1952, 1961.

The interaction of alter and ego gives rise to a social system. In its most elementary form this system consists of a set of mutual expectations. As ego has acted in the past so he is expected to act in the future. This is so with alter as well. A set of reciprocal expectations is established on the basis of the initial and continuing interaction. These expectations are selectively reinforced because rewarded actions are more likely to recur than unrewarded ones. The latter tend to drop out of the behavioural repertoire. Thus, from the continued interaction of alter and ego, and from their reciprocal expectations, social *roles* come to be differentiated. A role can be defined as a structured, normatively regulated participation by an individual in concrete interactions with specified, concrete role-partners. This implies that habitual interaction between two or more individuals quickly begets a system of *rules* which define permissible and anticipated behaviour patterns. These rules develop from the overall social necessity of ensuring the optimal gratification of emergent needs.

A complementary system of rights and duties attach themselves to the given roles: these arise out of the repeated satisfaction of expectations in an optimal way for the participants in the interaction. These special elements are summed up in norms or rules. The rules perform several functions: they define the limits of action; they specify rules of performance; they state the sanctions and rewards attached to performance of the role; they declare the particular situations or environments in which the role is acted out. If we have a plurality of actors operating according to an agreed set of rules which have the sanction of a system of social values, there we have a collectivity.[1]

The social system is not a mere conglomeration of roles, activities and collectivities. As behaviour is controlled by certain norms, so the whole complex of activities, roles and collectivities is governed by a value system.[2] Values are different from norms: for one thing, they have a greater degree of generality. The rules which appertain to a given set of roles are specific in character. In other words, they relate to particular situations and they refer to particular functions which the actors perform in the interest of the collectivity. On the other hand, values are

[1] Parsons, T. (1952), pp. 41, 97–8, 135–6, 174–5.
[2] Ibid., pp. 213–15, 263–4; (1961), pp. 43–4.

universal: at least they tend towards universality. They define the orientation of the system as a whole. This can be put in the form that values legitimize the activities of the whole social system. They tend to cluster around institutions: for example, there is a heavy concentration of values centred on the family, the economy, the State, and so on. Institutions, in fact, can be regarded as role-integrates.[1] They have a strategic relation to the need-system of the social group. As roles are on a low level of generality compared to institutions, so norms are lower in their level of generality than are values.

According to Parsons there are three kinds of social institution. At its very core the social system has *relational* institutions. These define reciprocal role-expectations. Some examples of relational institutions are: husband-wife, parent-child, employer-employee, and so on. Secondly there are *regulative* institutions. These operate to regulate the interests of individuals and collectivities by defining the legitimate means to be employed in the pursuit of interest. Examples are: the police, courts of law, the Stock Exchange, Parliament, and so on. Thirdly, there are *cultural* institutions. These define obligations in relation to culture patterns and act so as to orient the individual towards accepted patterns of social meaning. Examples of cultural institutions are: accepted values, organized knowledge, beliefs, standards of artistic value, and so on. These various kinds of institution operate in such a way as to stabilize roles and interactions between individuals. They crystallize in a tangible form the level of organization and the differentiations which the social system has achieved. Each institution specifies in a unique and special way the accepted values of the given society. It serves as a central locus—a kind of storehouse so to speak of social roles. Material and spiritual resources are generated, allocated, and utilised through the medium of social institutions. Concrete units in the form of individuals, activities, collectivities appear, become specialised, and cluster around institutions.

The social system exhibits the same characteristics as behaviour in general. Behaviour is goal-directed; it is adaptive; it is motivated; it is guided by symbolic processes. Exactly the same things may be said of society. All social systems function

[1] Parsons, T. (1952), pp. 36–45, 51–8; *et altera* (1961), p. 65.

in accordance with the four exigencies of goal-seeking, adaptation, motivation and symbolization. Society must provide for the utilization of the resources available to it: this means, *firstly*, that society must be adaptive. Individuals and groups in society must be able to recognize and be impelled towards certain ends perceived as possible gratifications of felt needs; that is, *secondly*, the group must be organized towards goal-attainment. The social unit must be preserved from disintegration by disruptive tendencies. Putting this otherwise, the specific patterns of

S_{A_l}	S_{A_a}	S_{G_a}	S_{G_l}
	S_A	S_G	
S_{A_g}	S_{A_i}	S_{G_i}	S_{G_g}
S_{L_g}	S_{L_i}	S_{I_i}	S_{I_g}
	S_L	S_I	
S_{L_l}	S_{L_a}	S_{I_a}	S_{I_l}

activities, beliefs and values of society must be guarded from violent and destructive change; that is, *thirdly*, a combination of processes must reinstate the latent patterns of order and work to maintain tension at a manageable level. The different social units must mutually adjust themselves to each other in a continuous way so that their contribution to the effective functioning of the system can be maximized; that is, *fourthly*, an integrative subsystem is needed to facilitate internal adjustments and to adapt the system to the demands of the changing external situation.

As has already been said, each subsystem is open in character. Each can be divided along exactly the same lines as the social system itself into adaptive, integrative, goal-attainment, and pattern-maintenance sub-sub-systems. These sub-classifications give rise to sixteen empty boxes. These must be filled with an empirical content drawn from real social action.

The key problems in accounting for the functioning of social systems thus resolves itself into the question of the inter-actions and inter-relationships of the adaptive, integrative, goal-attainment and pattern maintenance subsystems. Clearly, interchanges and interactions must be across the boundaries of the subsystems. Internal interchanges are theoretically possible across six boundaries: S_A/S_G, S_A/S_I, S_A/S_L, S_G/S_I, S_G/S_L, S_I/S_L as shown in the diagram. There will also be exchanges across the external boundaries of the social system and the environing systems of nature, personality and culture. These interchanges will not be considered in detail; Smelser has given an elaborate and empirically based account of them.[1] Exchange between the subsystems takes place across the particular boundary which separates the common subsector of each subsystem. That is, the area in which exchange takes place between, say, S_G and S_A is the *a* subsector of each subsystem. This makes such interchanges as the following theoretically possible (these are not exhaustive):

i. S_{A_a} ⟷ S_{G_a}

ii. S_{L_a} ⟷ S_{I_a}

iii. S_{G_g} ⟷ S_{I_g}

iv. S_{A_g} ⟷ S_{L_g}

v. S_{G_i} ⟷ S_{L_i}

vi. S_{I_i} ⟷ S_{A_i}

The question now arises: what in fact passes across the boundaries between the subsystems? The transfers are clearly *not* physical objects, nor are they behaviour of organisms. Sociological analysis does not deal with concrete objects but with abstractions. This particular section of Parsons' and Smelser's analytical scheme is not elaborated to the point where a very clear picture can be given of what actually *happens* within the

[1] Smelser, N. (1959), pp. xii + 440.

social system in the general case. The sixteen boxes have un-doubtedly been filled. But it is not clear how, and in what form, materials travel from one to another, what the boundary condi-tions are which encourage or permit of exchanges, how the rate and direction of flow can be determined under differently specified conditions, how the equilibrium within the subsystems comes to be disturbed in the first place, what the conditions of rest may be, and what are the repercussions throughout the system as a result of transfers across boundaries. These are empirical questions. Specific answers are obtained only by close study of a particular case of boundary interchanges.

It is clear that the inputs to the social system are specifically from the cultural system, the personality system and the behavioural organism system. There is no direct input from the physical environment. Interchanges with the environment, in the form of inputs and outputs, are via the behavioural organ-ism. The inputs consist of *codes* for the organization of informa-tion, *need-dispositions* (of which there are four: adequacy, security, conformity and nurturance) and *plastic potentiality*. From within the social system itself values are generated. These various kinds of resource are made available as a result of inter-actions of the social system with each of the other three systems. They enter the social system at specific points; namely, from the cultural system to the adaptive subsystem, from the personality system to the goal-attainment subsystem, from the behavioural organism to the integrative subsystem. The different resources travel across the boundaries of the open systems and are 'pro-cessed' by various mechanisms. Certain products are fed back across the external boundaries to the environing systems. This 'processing' takes place in the sphere of social action. Resources are made use of by individuals and collectivities, *not* by the social system as such. The social system is, in fact, merely an abstraction. The transforming of inputs into outputs, as well as the consumption of resources, takes place in close connection with social roles. As Parsons says:

'Utilization is essentially a process of successively more par-ticularized decision-making; action-opportunities, facilities and responsibilities are allocated more specifically at each step. The most broadly defined stages are the allocation to the collectivity, to the role, and to the task. The function of the collectivity is to define what is to be done; that of allocation to role, to define who is to do it; and that of the task level, how it is to be done.'[1]

These relationships can be summed up in a diagram. It should be remembered in looking at this abstract model of the social system that it is *individuals* and *collectivities* which interact in the physical sense.

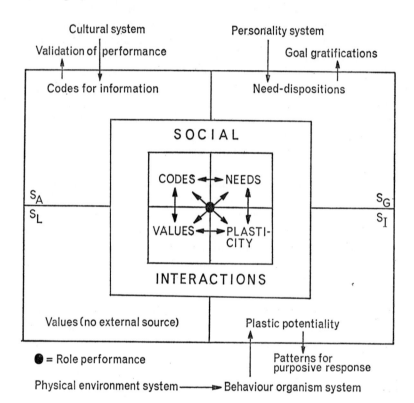

The Social System: Inputs and Outputs

The *end-result* of the utilization of resources within the social system is the accomplishment of tasks.[2] There are certain social mechanisms which control the flow and the processing of social resources and assist in ensuring the accomplishing of tasks.[3] Of

[1] Parsons, T. (1961), p. 65.   [2] Ibid., p. 65, *et altera.*
[3] Parsons, T. *et altera* (1961), pp. 52, 66.

these mechanisms, *money* has been subjected to the most detailed analysis. For Parsons, money is essentially a specialized mode of communication. Its social function is to act as a concrete representation in the circulation of expectations. It also acts to generate and to bind commitments to roles. Money assists in the rational allocation of resources: it has in it something of the nature of a social lubricant.

Closely analogous to money is the mechanism of *real commitment.*[1] Commitment to occupational roles (usually achieved through the money mechanism) enables realistic decisions to be made about the optimal use of resources. *Power* is another generalized social mechanism[2] which operates to legitimize expectations without a detailed advance statement of rights and obligations. Power helps in the process of adjusting conflicting interests within society: each side must consider and give due weight to the power disposed of by the other. The fourth mechanism which controls the flow and utilization of social resources is *communication.*[3] This takes several forms—information, interpretation, evaluation. These four social mechanisms operate as complex governors, or cybernetic controls which maintain the social system in a condition of dynamic equilibrium. Thus, according to Parsons, 'the dynamics of social systems is not so much a problem of the transformation of energy as of the processing of information'.[4]

The problem of social change arises when the equilibrium conditions, under which the system normally functions, are disturbed.[5] As is well known from physical science, equilibrium can be of three types: stable, partial, and unstable. In stable equilibrium, the system, when disturbed, returns to its original condition. In partial equilibrium, some units adjust, others do not. In unstable equilibrium, the system continually readjusts so that the elements occupy new positions within a constantly changing equilibrium.[6] In considering the social system, this scheme must be modified in several ways. No social system

---

[1] Ibid., pp. 66–7.
[2] Ibid., pp. 67–8; cf. (1952), pp. 55–7, 332.
[3] Ibid., p. 68; cf. (1952), pp. 30, 75, 121, 174–6.
[4] Ibid., p. 70; cf. (1952), pp. 33–5.
[5] Parsons, T. (1952), Chapter II; (1961), pp. 70–9.
[6] Bukharin, N. I. (1925), Chapters 4–7.

remains unaltered indefinitely, nor when disturbed does it return unaltered to its original state. The so-called 'stagnant' society is an 'ideal model' which simulates the conditions of stable equilibrium. There is constant replacement of everything needed for the smooth functioning of the system. Replacement takes place at exactly the same rate as the disappearance of units and resources. All productive forces, including the labour force, remain at the same level. Society moves neither backwards nor forward. This model nevertheless involves constant disturbances inasmuch as social products disappear as elements. It also involves the constant re-establishment of equilibrium inasmuch as the nascent social products assume their predestined place in the system.

Unstable equilibrium is the normal case. Growth, by differentiation and reduplication, is a factor which acts constantly to disturb social equilibrium. Growth entails changes and mutual adjustments in the elements of which the system is composed. The relationships between society and the external systems (nature, personality, culture) are dynamic, not static. If the system continues to develop it inevitably passes into a condition of unstable equilibrium, with positive indications.[1] On the other hand, equilibrium may be established at the expense of elements of the system. Segments coalesce, particular rules disappear. This leads in some cases to decreasing efficiency: the system fails to satisfy the needs of its members. In such cases we observe a system in decline, a condition of unstable equilibrium with negative indications.[2]

Equilibrium and change are complementary processes. Social change, according to Parsons[3] manifests itself first in the form of a boundary phenomenon. Its appearance is signalized by a breach in a boundary wall. This breakthrough brings into play various adjustment mechanisms which come into action in other parts of the system. Equilibrium is disturbed but control processes are called into operation to bring the system back into adjustment. In accordance with this model, the sources of change can readily be identified as either *endogenous* (that is, affecting boundaries within the system) or *exogenous* (that is, initiated from one of the systems outside the social system).[4]

[1] Bukharin, N I. (1925), Chapters 4–7.　[2] Ibid.
[3] Parsons, T. (1952), p. 482.　　　[4] Parsons, T. (1961), pp. 71–2.

In reality, both kinds of change work together. Exogenous changes rapidly produce endogenous changes: endogenous changes work outwards to change the external systems. This accords with the fact that society, personality, culture, and the physical organism are open systems in communication with each other. Endogenous changes in one system are identified as exogenous change-producing factors in the other systems. There are many kinds of exogenous changes which affect the social system—for example, genetic changes in the population; changes in the techniques of exploiting nature; the impact of other social systems, as in war, or in the form of cultural influences. These changes are external to the social system, but they have an impact on it. Endogenous changes are caused by 'strains' within the system itself. These strains result from certain disequilibria between inputs and outputs across the boundaries of subsystems. Several things can happen to these stresses and strains: they can be resolved, they can be arrested, they can be isolated, or they can be compensated for by changes in the structure of the system.[1]

Adjustments within the system will normally be associated with the reorganization of roles. This can take several forms, involving the disappearance, the creation or the modification of roles. Changes of this kind are more complex and continuous than changes where roles are not affected. Smelser recognizes a seven-fold sequence where the reorganization of roles leads to other kinds of structural differentiations within the system.[2] This does not mean that role differentiation is the *cause*, or *source*, of social change in the sense that the reorganization of roles has some priority of importance over other possible sources of change. According to Parsons, the concept of a system implies an interdependence of the elements or variables. This means that there is no predetermined causal sequence in the sense that some single over-riding factor is responsible for initiating change. The Marxist dichotomy of basis and superstructure is not regarded as useful by Parsons, nor does he locate the source of change in the economy. Analysis must determine in each case which is the leading factor, how the process develops, and how

[1] Ibid., cf. Parsons, T. (1952), pp. 36, 251, 482–3, 542–3.
[2] Parsons, T. and Smelser, N. (1957), especially pp. 252–61; Smelser, N. (1959).

change is transmitted through the parts of the social system. It is possible to recognize a hierarchy of importance amongst the factors which partake of the process of social change. The crucial focus lies in the value-system, according to Parsons. This is attested to by the fact that changes here have high impact on other systems.[1] But in any particular case the equilibrium conditions may be such that factors which are generally low in significance may be responsible for initiating change. The value system is a crucial focus only inasmuch as normally it is unaffected by slight changes in the system. Indeed values may, on occasion, be only marginally affected by quite large-scale innovations. In other circumstances, for example, a change of leadership, immediate and sharp changes in value-orientations may be produced: these may bring about profound and far-reaching consequences in the social system.

Social changes always have *impact*.[2] The nature of the impact depends on a number of factors. For example, there is a direct relationship between the impact and the magnitude of the change. Changes which have high impact involve a large number of units within the system. The magnitude of the impact depends very largely on the strategic significance of the units affected by change. For example, roles are readily affected by small changes; values are hardly affected even by large changes. To involve values in the process of change social innovations must be both large-scale and of high impact. This is shown by the fact that changes in values rapidly affect norms and work back through sub-collectivities to roles. Finally, the magnitude of the impact depends also on the resistance which results from the structural complexity of the system. The resistance which any given system can exert will depend on the amount of differentiation and segmentation within it. A highly differentiated system will be more capable of dispersing the impact of change than will a system consisting of but a small number of segments.

So far we have been dealing with an abstract sociological model. This has entailed leaving aside any consideration of the *people* involved in social action. It is, of course, human beings

[1] Parsons, T. (1961), pp. 72–4, 75–9, especially p. 78; cf. (1952), pp. 484–5, 498–9.
[2] Parsons, T. (1961), pp. 72–4.

who carry roles. Only *they* can act, hold steadfastly to value-systems, use resources, link society to the physical environment and allocate, utilize and consume resources. With regard to what might be considered as the objective need for social change it remains to be said that, in addition to other resistances to change, the *status quo* is embedded in the non-rational layers of their personality structure. Before change can take place ancient allegiances must be broken.

'The first prerequisite of change is disengagement from the preceding pattern. In other words, some order of relative deprivation becomes attached to following the old way. The impingement of the deprivation is on the individual and on the kinship collectivity. The impingement may take such forms as deterioration of previously assumed market conditions, or of the availability of new opportunities which cannot be utilized within the old structural framework. Such severe and prolonged relative deprivation would eventually give rise to symptoms of disturbance.[1]

Symptoms of disturbance are greater or less in extent according to the kind of support and permissiveness provided by the new, developing structure. Too great a pressure from the changing social system on individuals and groups, of a magnitude such as to force them to abandon their old ways totally and precipitately, may give rise to symptoms of marked psychological disturbance. Individuals, and groups as well, may become fixated on compulsive types of negative behaviour. Smelser has shown in his study of the Industrial Revolution that disturbance manifests itself as anxiety and aggression, in fantasies of Utopias and Arcadias, rebelliousness, withdrawal, and the ritualized, compulsive performance of roles. These symptoms accompanied various changes in family roles in spinning and weaving. Compulsive alienation and compulsive conformism are signs of disturbance which may appear when changes too great to be rapidly assimilated occur in the social system.[2]

The most profound social changes are associated with, and marked by, changes in the integrative subsystem. Such changes may be produced by outside factors. For example, religious

---

[1] Parsons, T. *et altera* (1961), p. 76.
[2] Smelser, N. (1959), especially Chapters 7–11.

beliefs may be taken over from some other group as the ascetic ideals of monasticism, through a process of secularization, gave rise to the Puritan ethic. Similarly, Nonconformist behaviour, ideals and beliefs over a period of time diffuse through a number of social systems.

There is another way in which social values can change, that is, from within. Within the system there is a profound resistance to change of values. The most general rules, norms, and values are those which are associated with religious belief. A prospective change, even the threat of change, in religious practices, values, or affiliations will normally be resisted to an extreme degree. Perhaps the only way open to a society to change its most profound beliefs from within is by charismatic innovation (Weber).[1] This means that a new leader, with a new doctrine and invested with wonder-working powers, or at least the appearance of them, must arise to proclaim the new truths. The new values become institutionalized in a new Church which sooner or later separates from the old. It is not enough simply to proclaim the new. The bearers of the charismatic truths must avoid at all costs being re-absorbed into the existing system of values if their insights are to be preserved. They may, on the other hand, subvert the older religious organization by infiltration from within. At this level value systems can also be changed by revolution. But this is a more difficult process which involves not only charismatic leaders but also the use of force.

Thus, for example, the significance of Puritanism in the Industrial Revolution lay in the fact that it had already appeared in precisely those areas and in the specific groups which later became involved in industrialization. As Weber pointed out, the Puritan ethic legitimized not only profit-making but also the instrumental use of human beings. The value system of the older community was overthrown *before* the economic, technological, political, and social revolutions associated with the factory system were completed. According to this view, the historical anticipation of social by religious change was a prerequisite of the relatively 'easy' progress of the Industrial Revolution in England.[2]

[1] Parsons, T. (1961), pp. 74–5 following Max Weber.

[2] Weber, M.: *The Protestant Ethic and the Spirit of Capitalism*, trans. T. Parsons.

In his elaborate study of this development Smelser recognizes seven stages in the process of social innovation. These are:

1. Dissatisfaction with role performance and with the utilization of resources;
2. Disturbance, which manifests itself in the forms of anxiety, aggression and fantasy;
3. Handling of dissatisfactions by mechanisms of social control, for example, the police or religious leaders;
4. A stage where new ideas are encouraged without responsibility falling on the innovators for implementing them;
5. Lines of action are specified with a view to commitment to a particular line of action;
6. These are tried out successively until success is assured;
7. Routinization of the new process, idea or value.[1]

[1] Smelser, N., op. cit., 1959.

5
THEORIES OF SOCIAL CHANGE: A COMPARATIVE ANALYSIS

The four theories of social change manifest several interesting similarities as well as quite striking differences. Once the theories have been grasped —at least so far as their basic tenets are concerned—the reader must himself confront the task of analysing their value as explanations of actual social changes. The writer does not regard it as his function to make up the reader's mind for him, but to indicate to him, and to help him use, some of the cognitive tools needed for the task of passing an informed judgement. To this end, it is of first priority to compare and contrast the theories with one another in a variety of ways.

Turning first to the basic similarities between the theories, we may consider:

(a) ORIGINS AND PURPOSES

It is interesting to note the origins of the four theories, especially in relation to their varying levels of generality.

The Marxist theory of social chance is integrally connected with a theory of social revolution. Indeed, it is not unfair to say that its main purpose was to provide a rationale for revolutionists. (Marx worked out the theory of dialectical materialism, fully conscious of the need for a rational, scientific and comprehensive basis for rejecting one particular kind of society namely, industrial capitalism. It was only after the theory had been elaborated as an intellectually polished system that he looked for empirical substantiation in the economic processes of capitalist society. His intuitive *enlargissement* of the views of earlier thinkers did not, of course, lack any empirical foundation. He was the residuary legatee of their analytic processing of their experience of social life. In addition, he had his own experience and analytical powers to guide him. But, as previously noted, his close associate, his alter-ego Engels admitted that historical materialism was not substantiated in even a single instance of historical change.)

Malinowski, on the other hand, developed functionalism as the theoretical end-product of a lengthy study of Melanesian society, with excursions into colonial Africa as a source of additional materials. Although functionalism has many intellectual forebears it carries many of the marks of an inductive generalization—much more than does Marxism. It is perhaps a defect of method in functionalism that the main data it was designed to explain are the materials of preliterate societies, that is, social organizations which have status systems but no class divisions. On the face of it, it would seem unlikely that functionalism would be relevant as an explanation of complex industrial societies. But it is not necessarily so. The general theory is of sufficient abstractness and generality to apply to *any* human community. It is, in fact, an attempt to define the common imperatives which arise from the association together of human beings and must be judged on that basis.

Parsons' view is grounded in the whole development of social thought from Machiavelli to the present day. He has the advantage over Marx, but not over Malinowski, that the empirical study of social origins and processes developed within the last few decades of the latter part of this period. Thus materials are available not only from highly developed, modern communities but from an intensive field study of preliterate and other kinds of human and animal groups. This material has not only been processed by the method of analytical abstraction (the method used also by Marx); included in it are observations and experiments carried out by psychologists, anthropologists and sociologists on the family, on working groups, on gangs, as well as on whole communities. An attempt has been made to evaluate Parsons' theory by trying to relate it to economic and social changes associated with the industrial revolution in England, as well as in other ways.

Taylor's theory is ultimately derived from the intensive investigation of mental illness by the method of psychoanalysis ('free association'). Various assumptions are made about the lack of any dividing line between the behaviour and psychic processes of neurotics and 'normal' people. Special hypotheses about the way in which infantile experience is assimilated and how it affects adult personality structures are used as the foundation for broad generalizations. An essentially medical technique (clinical intuition), of postulating a causal association between particular entities or processes is the methodological technique used in studying history and society. This technique implies that all other associations and processes are irrelevant. The idea that the extreme, unbalanced ('diseased') case can be the starting point from which we can begin to understand normal functioning is transferred from nosography to social diagnosis. The test of *objective reference*, that is, that we are speaking of *real* and not *imagined* connections, is certainly applied insofar as the historical record is ransacked for empirical data to support the hypotheses of nursery conditioning and of specific personality and behavioural types. But, as with Marx, the theory was fully elaborated from outside the area of theoretical study of social functioning, before any specialized study of social process was made. In the former case, the derivation was Hegel's philosophy, in the latter it was Freudian psychiatry.

(*b*) SCIENTIFIC STATUS

The four theories are clearly most suited to the study of trends, because of their high level of generality. As a converse, they do not seem so adequate as an explanation of the specific detail of historical and social events. Each has its own particular 'escape clauses' which enable special explanations of why particular social innovations do not proceed in accordance with the general model.

Marxism seems to be especially vulnerable to this criticism inasmuch as it declares that the economic basis will *in the long run* assert its influence as prime mover. This rather indefinite formulation, when combined with other statements, suggests that in reality everything accounts for everything else. Putting this otherwise, nothing accounts for anything. Malinowski makes the same assumption: that everything happens because it is necessary; if it doesn't happen this is proof that it wasn't really necessary. This circular argument is reminiscent of Galen's praise of Samian clay as a medical panacea:

'All who drink this remedy recover in a short time except those whom it does not help: these all die and have no relief from any other medicine. It is therefore obvious that this medicine fails only in incurable cases.'

The question is whether the various qualifications which are part of the more elaborate versions of these theories of social change are not of such a nature that they effectively remove the explanations entirely from the field of science into the realms of social mythology. The distinguishing mark of a scientific theory is that it is capable of empirical falsification. A theory should not be so flexible that it can never possibly be demonstrated to be wrong. Whilst it is true that all four theories can be used as a framework to support an *account* of particular cases of social change, this is hardly enough. A sociological theory is more than an abstract, general description of the possible connections between variables. Falsifiability is also an essential quality; otherwise we are speaking of something other than a scientific theory.

Smelser's account of social change (based on Parsons' theory) as proceeding in seven stages illustrates the point. According to Smelser, the seven stages need not succeed each other in an orderly sequence; regression is always possible, indeed likely. The sequence may be truncated by the omission of certain stages. Several sequences may occur together; or one sequence may be a compound of several. Not all sequences are complete, nor do all eventuate in social change. When these various qualifications have all been stated does anything at all remain of the original explanation? Similarly, Marx and Engels say that revolutions are produced by inherent contradictions in the economic basis which subsequently affect the superstructure of ideology. Then the following qualifications are added: that the superstructure, on occasion, takes the leading role and actively affects the basis; that contradictions within the superstructure are also capable of giving rise to basic innovations. What remains of the theory of historical materialism after these amendments? Again, Taylor informs us that thick-walled anal patrists may develop into thin-walled oral matrists. But he makes no attempt to define the conditions which produce these changes. Are we not being given a mere *description* of social changes in a rather eccentric terminology? Should not social theories provide that general explanation in terms of scientific causality implicit in the fact that they exist at all? Functionalism is not exempt from this criticism. The question here is: does the great variety of 'imperatives' in Malinowski's scheme not adequately account, but again essentially in descriptive terms, for all possible types of social behaviour? Is functionalism nothing more than the old, discredited, circular explanation of social behaviour in terms of 'instinct' with only the *word* 'instinct' left out?

(c) DETERMINISM AND THE PLACE OF THE INDIVIDUAL

All four theories accept the principle of determinism so far as social processes and individual responses are concerned.

Marxism leaves room for the passionate, partisan, class-fighter. But his freedom lies in the recognition of necessity. Unless he has the vision of a god, or of Marx himself, unless he understands the movement of history, the shifting alignments and conjunctions of class forces, unless he appreciates the contradictions in productive forces and their actual development, his efforts to change society must be in vain. In any case, the consequences of his individual action are lost in that massive resolution of forces and intentions which constitutes the social process.

In Malinowski's scheme the *needs of the group* have the same over-riding character. The contribution of the individual is always within an institutional framework which places a premium on conformism. Social innovation may be the result of a spontaneous endogenous evolution: more commonly, however, it is the result of a confrontation between native and intrusive cultures. As we have seen above, there is an interaction between exogenous, i.e. intrusive, and endogenous, i.e. native culture patterns, according to the functionalist explanation of change. Cooperation, conflict or compromise between the two cultures results. But whatever happens is the outcome of a social decision which is determined by definite forces and resistances. Culture is not just a heap of opportunities from which the innovator can freely take what he likes. An inner determinism is imposed by the equilibrium conditions of the social system. Similarly, when cultures interact the character of the borrowings is not arbitrarily determined. There is a lawful process of change in which the human agent participates, but passively rather than actively.

In Parsons' explanatory scheme the individual is not even

the unconsidered unit of a vastly more interesting system, as he is for Malinowski. In fact, sociologically speaking, the individual has no real existence: the social system does not consist of individuals at all. It is composed of roles and actions. These are carried, or perpetrated, by individuals. No doubt there is always a certain latitude in the playing of a particular role. Social actions cannot ever be prescribed in an absolute form. But the individual style which is expressed in the way the role is played or the social act carried out is, itself, the resultant of other kinds of determinant. In Parsons' system innovations result from breaches in the boundary walls between systems or subsystems. These breaches call forth attempts to restore equilibrium. It is, no doubt, individuals who show the various signs of disturbance (aggression, anxiety, fantasy). Ideas are produced and tried out by human beings: emotions are expressed in individual behaviour. But it is 'the system' which is decisive. Initiative lies in the boundary-processes which restore equilibrium.

In Taylor's theory of change, paternal images are the prime movers of social action. The image begins to form during the tenderest years of infancy, outside of consciousness and awareness. The anal patrist can find convincing explanations for his beliefs and behaviour, so can the oral matrist. But these explanations are merely the result of the interplay between a general abstracting ability which human beings possess, their ego-needs, and animal impulses. In other words, they are rationalizations. Social behaviour itself is essentially irrational: individual and social behaviour has little real connection with expressed intention or any rational decision process. No matter what convincing and apparently rational reasons may be found for social change, the participants are at the mercy of what are, to them, unknown and uncontrollable forces.

All four theories therefore reduce the status of the social agent or innovator. Each does it in characteristic fashion. None allows to the innovator the possibility of realizing his intention in exactly the form he desires. In no case is he fully aware of the nature of the process in which he is involved. According to Marxist theory the 'agent' works all the time under certain systematic delusions. His ideas have a topsy-turvy relation to the dialectical processes in which he is, willy-nilly, involved. He has a consciousness which falsely 'reflects' reality: he remains necessarily unaware of the real source and consequences of his actions. The proletarian 'agent', no less than other protagonists, is involved in a 'sham' fight with opponents whom he can scarcely even identify. But through this shadow-boxing certain crucial relations become clear: eventually he may become aware of his true interests. However, he remains dependent on someone else (the middle-class intellectual who is not actively involved in the struggle) to formulate his ideas clearly and to develop a consistent policy for his whole social class. In Malinowski's theory, man's basic needs are certainly primary. But they express themselves in a social form and can be satisfied only within the same context. In fact, function over-rides everything: the individual must give way to the social imperatives. In Parsons' theory, the human being takes the stage as a mere 'actor', playing a role in accordance with the expectations of others. His actions, his role, his value-system, the rules of life which hedge him in, are fixed according to his place in the social system. The external systems of nature, culture, society press in on him. To these he must counterpose his own social action. He does not, and cannot, freely choose his stance nor point of pressure but must accept a pre-ordained place and role. The individual behaves as one element in a vast system: he as well as it are controlled by forces of which he necessarily remains unaware. In Taylor's theory man is a kind of knot or vortex of libidinal energy, a mere plaything of blind, unconscious impulses which have him in their grip. Essentially he is a victim: through his nursery experience his parents have made him what he is, a creature of habit and unconscious complex, with a certain degree of spontaneity which is determined by the blind impersonal forces and counter-forces of libido and environment.

(d) LEVELS OF GENERALIZATION

Another respect in which the theories agree is that each is part of a highly developed general theory. In discussing social innovation Marxism proceeds from the highest level of abstraction, that of the cosmic process. Social behaviour is one aspect of matter in motion. It conforms to the general laws of dialectics which apply to systems everywhere. Although we must investigate individual cases to discover the *specific* characteristics of phenomena, the general framework of method and even the nature of the findings are already determined in broad outline. In the case of Malinowski's theory, social change finds a place already prepared for it in the general theory of functionalism. The contact situation within which culture-change is generated must be approached as an integral whole. The unit of analysis remains the institution. The investigator is involved in tracing how some institutions change, how others persist, what the charter of the new institutions may be, what the function of the new order of things is. In Parsons' theory, the problem of social change is answered by applying the general theory of action systems. In terms of the principles of systems-analysis much is known before we even investigate the problem. The necessary postulates and concepts are already provided through which change can be assimilated to the general theory. In the case of Taylor, lying behind his special theories is an elaborate body of knowledge based on the use of a special method. This knowledge provides a general supporting framework for the special explanations, already half-way formulated before the field is even surveyed in a preliminary canter. Freud's theories of unconscious motivation need no special development to be applied to social action, according to the theory. Indeed no fundamental distinction can be made between behaviour and social action. No man is ever fully alone; there is always at least one other subjectively present, as model, as rival, or as erotic object. Freud himself declares that the distinction between individual and social psychology is false: *all* psychology is social psychology.

(e) SOURCES OF AND RESISTANCES TO SOCIAL CHANGE

Whilst recording certain qualifications, each theory locates the source of change in some special part of the total system. This subsystem, whatever it be, is credited with playing rather a special part in initiating and guiding change. In some sense or other it operates in such a way as to validate the particular changes which have taken place. In Marxism the economy plays this leading role. Contradiction—between productive forces and productive relations, or in the production process

77

itself, engenders change. The whole system, basis and super-structure, adjusts in a direction determined by the relations be-tween the vital elements of the economic basis. In Malinowski's theory the crucial focus is human needs and their satisfaction. The cultural system adapts to vital needs by a process like natural selection. The fundamental law is that the social system must provide for the optimal satisfaction of basic imperatives. There is, of course, a hierarchy even with reference to needs ('man does not live by bread alone, but he lives primarily by bread'). In Parsons' system role differentiation is the prime measure and manifestation of change. The process, which starts here, soon involves the whole functioning system. According to Taylor, the leading role is played by infant rearing practices. It is human personality which makes history: but personality itself is the product of permissive or restrictive nursery régimes.

All four theories recognize built-in resistances to change. Marxism perceives these as being based on the need to defend class interests and class gains. But resistances must also be ex-plained on a deeper level. Marx points to a general process of resurgence and decay, that is, at any given moment certain forces are developing while others are passing away. The process of change is based on the dialectical opposition between those forces which represent the new and those which represent the old. The successful innovator is he who is able to perceive which forces are on the side of progress and which are dying away. He must be in the position of giving effective support to the former while opposing the latter.

Malinowski is not so apt as Marx to recognize, or at least to describe, the resistances to change. The normal source of innovation for functionalism lies in the impact of one culture on another. The typical phenomena associated with culture clash are the adoption, the rejection, or the transformation of certain institutions, along with the development of new ones. The contact of two cultures results in cooperation, conflict, or compromise. It may be presumed that in the normal case there is, in fact, a mixture of all three responses, with a predominance of one or other at different stages. Malinowski seems to accept the model of equilibrium and adjustment as an analogue of the cultural system. We find this model, more highly developed, also in Parsons. Change, according to the action theory, marks a deviation from some given set of initial conditions. With the disturbance of these equilibrium conditions there ensues a period of maladjustment, deterioration, social strain, confusion. These conflict phenomena are indicative of the onset of change and of the reactions of those forces which are resistant to it. In fact, Parsons gives an account which is essentially very similar to that of Malinowski, of the disturbance of equilibrium conditions, with consequent aggression, anxiety and fantasy. In addition to these specific reactions, Parsons recognizes other boundary processes which are mobilized initially to prevent any disturbance or to reinstate the earlier equilibrium conditions.

In Taylor's theory, the resistance to change is located in certain kinds of personality structure. Instead of a clash between cultures Taylor sees only a conflict between persons. That particular personality structure which integrates father-identification with the obsessional traits of the anal personality fears and resists change of any kind. In fact, the traits of obstinacy, parsimony and orderliness (which Freud associated as the major components of the anal personality) can be thought of as unconscious defences which are erected against any threat to the introjected internal objects, especially that of the father-image. The thick-walled ego is also a defence against dynamic forces from the environment which continue to threaten the integration of the psyche. The spontaneous, uninhibited oral matrist represents the polar opposite of the anal-patrist change-resister. According to this theory, these two personality types should be most sharply in conflict in a situation of rapid social change. In such a situation they will confront each other, the former appearing as the ultra-conservative, the latter as the enemy of the established order.

(f) SOURCES OF CHANGE INTERNAL TO THE SYSTEM

All four systems are ready to recognize the possibility of change due to movement *within* the system. In Marxism, endogenous processes are considered to be the normal vehicle of change. There is a maturing of the new within the womb of the old. This maturation process proceeds by the accumulation of small quantitative differences: this cumulative phase eventually reaches some kind of limit when there ensues a sharp, qualitative change.

The old passes away simultaneously with the birth of a new thing. In social change evolutionary transformation necessarily prepares the ground for revolution. Both are essential ingredients of the on-going process of dialectical change. Malinowski also recognizes a slow process of evolutionary change. But he seems inclined to regard most innovations as the result of diffusion from peripheral cultures, rather than as the product of endogenous processes. In Parsons' theory change from within takes the form of 'charismatic innovation'. This entails marked changes, normally in the religious values of a community, changes produced through the instrumentality of some prophet of power who arises to denounce the old way and point to the new. Taylor emphasizes the possibility of a slow secular change in paternal images. The source of this change is not made clear, but it is plain that it must be the result of personal influence. This would imply a long-drawn-out process of individual conversion to new attitudes, to child rearing and other associated activities, taking place in society. The transition, still following Taylor, will normally be associated with economic and social changes. These operate to bring novel attitudes and techniques into prominence so that they are imitated by large numbers of people. It seems probable that this kind of change is to be explained as the result of pendulum-like swings of fashion: the swings can be interpreted as action followed by reaction, one extreme begetting its opposite, in an endless sequence of irrational movements.

These are some similarities between the four theories: they stand or fall together on these questions. But in assessing the value of each theory as an analytical tool, emphasis must now be laid on the differences between them. The special virtues and defects of each can be highlighted in this way, and a basis laid for rational choice between them.

(I) METHODOLOGICAL DIFFERENCES

The first thing to be said is that a different method is used in establishing and evaluating hypotheses. All four systems use a scientific method in studying social reality; but there are important differences in how this method is used.

(Marx employs the _dialectical_ method, a method which is essentially critical and revolutionary. He consciously sets out to grasp the inner contradictions of a given historical situation; this provides the key to the whole social movement. Social development is treated as strictly analogous to natural evolution. It is assumed that human society is governed by laws which are not only independent of our will, consciousness and intelligence, but which determine that will, consciousness and intelligence.)It is a guiding principle of Marxism, that scientific laws themselves are not invariable being, like everything else, subject to the universal processes of change. In these two basic principles Marxism differs in method from all other systems of social analysis. The Marxist must look at every social stage with fresh eyes since each has its own laws of change which must be discovered afresh.

Malinowski's method is _functionalist_. Like Marx, he excludes speculations about human motives as irrelevant, concentrating on objectively determinable factors, especially on the leading determinants of social systems. Man, society and culture represent a single entity: each can only be understood in relation to the other two. To dissociate them is to remove the context which gives _meaning_ to the analysis and to fore-doom the result. His approach depends on the assumption that culture is an instrumental apparatus which enables man to solve the concrete and highly specific problems which confront him in his environment, primarily those which have to do with the satisfaction of his needs. Everything social is examined from this point of view, since this is the basic law of all human societies.

Parsons uses the method of _analytical abstraction_ to deduce a system of postulates and propositions about social systems. His ultimate aim would appear to be to arrive at a hypothetico-deductive framework of propositions which will explain social processes as a special case of the general laws of action systems. His analysis of the social system runs in parallel with other studies—of the family, the economic system, certain historical events, changes within small groups, and so on. The same variables are recognized, similar processes are identified.

Taylor uses a _biographical_ method: his emphasis lies on the first few years of life which are regarded as crucial both for individual development and hence for social processes. The

81

method is *reductionist* in that social events are conceptualized in terms of an interplay between biological factors and certain features of individual destiny. The basic explanatory concepts are: the predominance of unconscious factors in determining social attitudes and behaviour; the inheritance by human beings of particular constellations of unconscious ideas and impulses, in particular the Oedipus complex; the opposition between the biological and the social needs of human beings; the development of the personality by differentiation from an originally homogenous knot of libidinal energy. The method used to establish the postulated relations between childhood experiences and social attitudes is anecdotal and analogical.

(2) PREDICTIVE ACCURACY AND POWER

The theories differ in predictive power. The Marxist system is characterized by a strong tendency towards highly generalized predictions on a grand scale. It is notorious that the time scale of these predictions needs continually to be revised as certain kinds of social systems show powers of resistance to predicted change far beyond Marxist expectation. With regard to local predictions of small-scale political and social changes, these are usually so highly coloured by hope and propagandist intent that they can hardly be taken seriously as belonging in the realm of scientific predictions at all. Malinowski's system comes under the same strictures—perhaps more even than those passed on Marxism. The predictive power of his theory is virtually zero. The explanation of any cultural phenomenon is so highly generalized that it explains everything in general, but at the same time nothing specifically. Interpretation of change must always be *ex post facto* as far as Malinowski is concerned.

In Parsons' system we have a highly detailed scheme with which to interpret successive stages of change. We are also provided with a working model of the way in which change proceeds from one level to another—from activities, to roles, to norms, to values, and vice-versa. The ease with which Parsons' scheme can be transferred, with only nominal modifications, from one field of sociological investigation to another gives it high predictive value.

Taylor just fails to provide the kind of analysis which enables

82

predictions to be made: he moves on the same level of abstraction and generality as does the Marxist system. It is perhaps possible, with him, to recognize trends which can be described as patrist and matrist. These can probably be linked up with one or other predominant nursery régime. But no rule is stated which would enable us to forecast the duration of phases. Nor are we told anything of the conditions which ensure that one régime will predominate rather than another, nor do we know the factors which lead to the substitution of one parental image by another. It is not at all clear how it happens that only two or three well-marked types of personality predominate, to the exclusion of dozens of other possible types.

(3) LOGICAL STRUCTURE

Internal coherence is another quality which distinguishes the four theories. This can be defined as the number of basic constructs required by the system, and the logical relationships that exist between them. By definition, the greater the number of qualifying hypotheses involved in an exposition of the system, the lower is the degree of internal coherence.

Judged by this criterion the Marxist theory of social change does not show a very high order of coherence. On the other hand, functionalism does. The number of basic concepts is low. They are specified with great clarity so far as the indication of objective realities is concerned. In other words their potential 'fit' to empirical reality seems to be much closer. They show a close logical relatedness, forming an interlocking system of postulates. They are adequate in themselves, without supplementary processes and explanations. In comparison, the internal coherence of Parsons' theory is low. The distinction between integrative and pattern-maintenance, between adaptive and goal attainment subsystems is hard to maintain. This kind of segmentation of the social system involves overlapping and repetition: the 'fit' of the concepts to underlying reality does not seem very close. The psychoanalytic system in Taylor's modification clearly exhibits a high degree of internal consistency. Few logical constructs are needed to define the system and these are closely integrated. There is a clearly defined relationship between the analytical constructs and the objective realities with which they deal. This does not necessarily imply a correspondence in fact, merely that the path from logical construct to reality is a short one, requiring few intervening steps.

(4) CONCEPT OF THE SOCIAL SYSTEM

Finally, let us consider the nature of the total picture of the social system with which each theory presents us. Three of the four theories involve the conception of a system in equilibrium. In Marxism, capitalism is conceptualized as a system constantly reproducing itself, at the same time as it is constantly growing. But growth, although continuous, is not regular in all parts of the system. This periodically leads to a breakdown in equilibrium signalized by crises of overproduction. However, the system has great powers of recuperation, so that equilibrium is very soon reestablished. The system is guaranteed to survive until that particular arrangement appears which is able to develop the productive resources to the maximum level possible. A new system then develops out of the old, with new elements and a novel arrangement of the parts. This new system is also in unstable equilibrium and, in its time, doomed to disappear. In Malinowski's theory we find a very similar state of affairs. But the equilibrium is of a more stable kind, without crises, and without unequal development. The system alters from within, certainly. But the greatest alterations are produced by the intrusion of materials from the external systems. Change is not the consequence of a radical breakdown of the system, as in the Marxist formulation. Rather there is a process of gradual and relatively peaceful assimilation at the edges (the word 'diffusion' is appropriately used). Parsons' model is based entirely on the concept of an equilibrium state. The social system is subject to periodical innovations from internal rearrangements, segmentations, coalescences, destructions, and so on.

On the other hand, Taylor has no developed conception of the social system: for him it is a mere heterogeneous collection of individuals, perhaps stratified by class, certainly responding to personal influences in the course of socialization processes which are completed in childhood. It is true that Freud himself elaborated a model of the individual as a system operating on the basic principle of economy of psychic energy, and that he visualized the unconscious as an adjustive system which controls behaviour. But this psychoanalytic conception of the equilibrium system has not been extended to society by Taylor. A system, whether in equilibrium or not, consists of various elements. Marx distinguishes between productive forces and productive relations, between economic basis and ideological superstructure. Within each category further elements can be distinguished. If we were to make a detailed inventory, it would soon be clear that Marx accepts the categories of everyday life (factories, workers, money, tools, time, raw materials, commodities and so on) as the elements of his system. He is involved in the attempt to formulate abstract laws which relate these entities to each other. In the case of Malinowski, his categories are down-to-earth in quite the same way. The cultural system is composed of activities, personnel, artefacts, norms, functions, charters, material apparatus. These categories each contain objectively observable materials or behaviour. Parsons, on the other hand, does not deal in tangible realities. The 'functional imperatives' (pattern-maintenance, integration, adaptation and goal-attainment) are abstractions. The ancillary flow mechanisms (money, power, real commitments, communication) are also immaterial abstractions, at least so far as their social function and appearance are concerned. In the psychoanalytic theory there is no attempt to make an analysis of society. It remains largely undifferentiated, except in terms of individual personalities and broad social classes.

The concept of a system in equilibrium involves the notion of control mechanisms. In the Marxist theory the main mechanism of control, under capitalism, is the market. The standard of value is determined by the amount of socially necessary labour time incorporated in a given commodity. This criterion operates at the point when the commodity reaches the market: there the laws of supply and demand act to fix prices. Ultimately the functioning of the whole system revolves around this process of production and exchange. Under Malinowski's functionalism, the control of innovation, and of the total system in general, is effected through the mechanism of basic and derived needs. Similarly, Parsons points to the 'functional imperatives' as the major controls which act to maintain the system in equilibrium. In this analytic scheme there are other homeostatic mechanisms: one may instance money, power, communication, vital commitments. These keep the system running smoothly. The whole social process is governed by the value system which acts to legitimize and define activities. In Taylor's psychoanalytic scheme the controls on behaviour bear the character of defence mechanisms. An elaborate body of theory has been built up around the notion that the ego must defend itself against animal impulses from within and from a hostile environment without. But the theory has not, so far, been generalized to group behaviour in such a way as would repay comparison with the other systems. The work of Bion (and the method of group psychotherapy) may perhaps be referred to, without elaboration, at this point.

The concept of a 'social system' necessarily involves the idea of interchanges between its various parts. In the theory of historical materialism there are various kinds of interchange. For example, we can categorize the system in terms of productive forces and productive relations. In the normal running of the system there will be a close connection between the form of productive relations and the degree of development of the productive forces. They mutually influence each other. According to Marx, the level of development of the productive forces determines both the type of social system and the nature of productive relations within it: whether it be a capitalist, or feudal, or slave-owning or socialist society depends on the level of development of production. It is a basic premise of Marx that as the productive forces grow they come into conflict with the productive relations. To take but one example: at a particular stage of growth of the economic basis, slave-owning becomes relatively unproductive and unprofitable. The productive relations (of master and slave) then act as fetters on further production. The maturing productive forces burst the old integument of slave society: a new society, with new productive relations, comes into being. In addition to relations of antagonism and concomitant development, Marxism recognizes the relationship of 'reflection' as between systems. The ideological superstructure reflects the economic basis. Changes in the economy are paralleled by changes in the state, in law, in religion, in science, and so on. But, it must be said that the way in which 'reflection' takes place has never been worked out, even in the most general sense.

Malinowski does not differentiate subsystems within the cultural system, nor does he consider how interchanges might take place. But it appears as if a connection could easily be made out between the integrative imperatives (knowledge, religion and magic) and (say) the economic activities of the community. To take but one example: the symbolizing process is clearly at work in magic ritual where the action is representative of the desired effect, as in rain-making ceremonies. Frazer's distinction between 'contagious' and 'sympathetic' magic comes to mind at this point. The dance mimics the hunt, the initiation ceremonies belong to both the instrumental (educational, political, normative and economic) and to the integrative group of imperatives. All cultural imperatives are closely related to the basic imperatives. These connections have not been elaborated by Malinowski.

In Parsons' scheme there is a constant interchange across the boundaries of subsystems. Indeed, this is the conception at the heart of the action theory and, in the opinion of some, might be the factor to tip the balance in its favour.

BIBLIOGRAPHY

Bales, R. F. *Interaction Process Analysis: A Method for the Study of Small Groups.* Addison-Wesley, Cambridge, Mass., 1950.

Barnett, H. G. *Innovation: the Basis of Cultural Change.* McGraw-Hill Book Co., N.Y., 1953.

Black, M. (Ed.) *The Social Theories of Talcott Parsons.* Prentice-Hall, Englewood Cliffs, N.J. 1961.

Dobbs, A. E. *Education and Social Movements, 1700–1850.* Longmans, Green & Co., 1919.

Dollard, J., *et al. Frustration and Aggression.* Kegan Paul, 1944: Yale U.P., New Haven, 1939.

Ellis, A. and Abarbanel, A. (Eds.) *Encyclopaedia of Sexual Behaviour.* 2 vols. Hawthorn Books, N.Y., 1961.

Freud, S. *Character and Anal-Erotism* (1908). *Collected Papers,* Vol. 2, pp. 45–50. Hogarth Press, 1949.

Freud, S. *Collected Papers,* Hogarth Press, 1949: Basic Books, N.Y., 1949.

Freud, S. *Complete Works,* Hogarth Press, 1953: Macmillan, N.Y., 1953.

Freud, S. *The Unconscious* (1915). *Collected Papers,* Vol. 4, pp. 98–136. Hogarth Press, 1949.

Freud, S. *The Relation of the Poet to Daydreaming. Collected Papers,* Vol. 4, pp. 173–83. Hogarth Press, 1949.

Freud, S. *The Moses of Michelangelo* (1914). *Collected Papers,* Vol. 4, pp. 257–287. Hogarth Press, 1949.

Freud, S. *Three Essays on Sexuality* (1905). *Complete Works, Standard Edition,* Vol. 7, pp. 125–245. Hogarth Press, 1953.

Freud, S. *The Interpretation of Dreams* (1900). *Complete Works, Standard Edition,* Vols. 4 and 5. Hogarth Press, 1953.

Freud, S. *Leonardo da Vinci and a Memory of his Childhood, 1910. Complete Works, Standard Edition,* Vol. 11, pp. 59–137. Hogarth Press, 1957.

Freud, S. *Der Witz und Seine Beziehung zum Unbewussten* (1905). *Complete Works, Standard Edition,* Vol. 8. Hogarth Press, 1960.

Healy, W. and Bronner, A. F. *The Structure and Meaning of Psychoanalysis.* Knopf, N.Y., 1949.

Hecker, J. F. *Russian Sociology.* Chapman & Hall, 1934.

Homans, G. C. *The Human Group.* Routledge & Kegan Paul, 1950: Harcourt Brace & World, N.Y., 1950.

Kammari, M. D. *Socialism and the Individual.* Moscow, 1952.

Kinsey, A. and Pomeroy, W. B. *Sexual Behaviour in the Human Male.* Saunders, Philadelphia, 1948.

Konstantinov, F. V. *The Role of Socialist Consciousness in the development of Soviet Society.* Moscow, 1950.

Konstantinov, F. V. *Role of Advanced Ideas in Development of Society.* Moscow, 1954.

BIBLIOGRAPHY

Konstantinov, F. V. *Basis and Superstructure.* Moscow, 1955.

Lenin, V. I. *Filosofskiye Tetradi.* Moscow, 1938.

Lenin, V. I. *Cahiers Philosophiques.* Editions Sociales, Paris, 1955.

Lenin, V. I. *Sochineniya.* 4th edition, 35 volumes. Moscow, 1941–1950.

Lenin, V. I. *The Development of Capitalism in Russia.* Moscow, 1957.

Malinowski, B. *Sex and Repression in Savage Society.* Kegan Paul, Trench, Trubner, London, 1937: Humanities Press, N.Y., n.d.

Malinowski, B. *The Dynamics of Culture Change.* Yale U.P., New Haven, 1945.

Malinowski, B. *A Scientific Theory of Culture.* Galaxy edition. Oxford U.P., 1960.

Martindale, D. *Social Life and Cultural Change.* Van Nostrand, Princeton, N.J., 1962.

Marx, K. and Engels, F. *Briefwechsel 1844–1883.* 4 vols. Ring-Verlag, Zurich, 1935.

Marx, K. and Engels, F. *Marxist Leninist Library.* 20 vols. Lawrence & Wishart, London, 1936–1940.

Meijer, J. M. *Knowledge and Revolution,* Van Gorcum, Assen, 1955: Humanities Press, N.Y., 1965.

Morison, E. E. 'A Case Study of Innovation'. In *Frontiers in Science,* ed. Edward Hutchings, Jun. Basic Books, N.Y., 1958.

O'Connor, N. and Francks, C. M. 'Childhood Upbringing and other environmental factors. In Eysenck, H. J. (Ed.): *Handbook of Abnormal Psychology,* pp. 393–416. Pitman, London, 1960: Basic Books, N.Y., 1961.

Parsons, T. *The Social System.* Tavistock Publishers, London, 1952: Free Press, Glencoe, Ill., 1951.

Parsons, T. *Essays in Sociological Theory.* Glencoe Free Press, Glencoe, Ill., 1954.

Parsons, T. 'Pattern Variables Revisited: a Response to Robert Dubin'. *Am. Soc. Rev.,* 1960, **25,** 467–83.

Parsons, T. *Structure and Process in Modern Societies.* Glencoe Free Press, Glencoe, Ill., 1959.

Parsons, T. and Shils, E. A. *Toward a General Theory of Action.* Harvard U.P., Cambridge, Mass., 1951.

Parsons, T., *et al. Family, Socialization and Interaction Process.* Free Press, Glencoe, Ill., 1955. Routledge & Kegan Paul, 1955.

Parsons, T. and Smelser, N. J. *Economy and Society.* Routledge & Kegan Paul, 1957.: Free Press, Glencoe, Ill., 1956.

Parsons, T., *et al. Theories of Society.* 2 vols. Free Press, Glencoe, Ill., 1961.

Plekhanov, G. V. *The Role of the Individual in History.* Moscow, 1946. International Publishers, N.Y. n.d.

Rieff, P. *Freud: The Mind of the Moralist.* Methuen University Paperback, 1961: Anchor Books, N.Y., 1961.

Smelser, N. J. *Social Change in the Industrial Revolution.* Routledge & Kegan Paul, London, 1959: University of Chicago, 1959.

Smelser, N. J. *Theory of Collective Behaviour.* Routledge & Kegan Paul, London, 1962: Free Press, Glencoe, Ill., 1962.

Taylor, G. R. *The Angel-Makers.* Heinemann, London, 1958: Verry, Lawrence, Mystic, Conm., 1958.

BIBLIOGRAPHY

Taylor, G. R. *Sex in History*. Thames, London, 1954: Vanguard Press, N.Y., 1954.

Troeltsch, E. *The Social Teaching of the Christian Churches.* 2 vols. Allen & Unwin, 1931.

Venable, V. *Human Nature: The Marxian View.* Dennis Dobson, London, 1946: Meridan Books, N.Y., n.d.

NAME INDEX

SUBJECT INDEX